Praise for *Served in Silence*

"When you hear a voice speaking the truth, their unique and personal truth, it's like being surrounded by the most perfectly tuned chimes excited by the wind and hearing only that pure sound. You are in, and with a divine presence. Mark's moment was hearing his own voice and now he's sharing it with us. This generous and intimate authenticity is rare. Reading his memoir, *Served in Silence*, will change you."

—*Sam McClure*
Senior Vice President
National LGBT Chamber of Commerce® (NGLCC)

"As an author I aspire to capture the authenticity of the characters in my stories and demonstrate their struggles. In his memoir, *Served in Silence*, Mark David Gibson has brilliantly captured and identified the hazards of functioning outside of one's authentic self, while highlighting the success of a genuine life. Although repressed by the military's Don't Ask, Don't Tell policy, Gibson takes you on his journey to survive and inspires all of us to embrace our truths."

—*Phyllis H. Moore, Author*

"*Served in Silence* is victorious and enlightening. I have known Mark for over 20 years and have experienced most of what he writes about in his memoir. Like many of us struggling to live authentically, Mark lost his way. One of the most incredible things I have witnessed in my life is his courage, tenacity, and strength to find his way back, which we call Mark 2.0. I was with him during the Don't Ask, Don't Tell years and later helped him conquer his addiction to alcohol. *Served in Silence* draws focus on the very essence and fabric of hope, love, and authentic friendships."

—Major Bryn A. Russell, USAF, Retired

"When President Obama tasked my agency to be more inclusive to the LGBT community, I developed an economic empowerment outreach strategy: the Many Faces One Dream tour and the Harvard award-winning LGBT Business Builder. In his memoir, *Served in Silence,* you will see why I chose Mark Gibson as our National Communications Director. Mark's dedication, loyalty, passion and over-the-top enthusiasm are the exact qualities we needed for this initiative. He leads by example and exemplifies these traits."

—Eugene Cornelius, Jr.
Deputy Associate Administrator for International Trade
U.S. Small Business Administration

"Like Mark David Gibson, I believe that one of the essential keys to success is embracing the diverse cross-sections of our identity and striving to live authentically. Gibson's memoir, *Served in Silence,* provides a tremendous example. Working with college students, my hope is that they may, like Mark, defy the odds and overcome obstacles resulting in a positive, productive, and successful life."

—E. Gerome Stephens, Ph.D.
Associate Dean of Students
Georgia Institute of Technology

"I was honored to serve in the United States Air Force with Captain Mark Gibson and proud to call him my dear friend. I have had a front row seat to Mark's life and have personally witnessed this inspirational journey for more than 20 years. Mark's courage to tell his story in his memoir, *Served in Silence,* will serve as a beacon of hope for anyone struggling to live authentically and conquer the battle of "service to country" above "service to self." Bravo Captain Gibson, bravo!"

— Lieutenant Colonel Johnny F. Ginnity, USAF, Retired

Served in Silence

Served in Silence

The Struggle To Live Authentically

Mark David Gibson

PUBLISH
YOUR
PURPOSE
PRESS

For permission requests, write to the publisher, addressed "Attention: Permissions Coordinator," at the address below.
Publish Your Purpose Press
141 Weston Street, #155
Hartford, CT 06141

The opinions expressed by the Author are not necessarily those held by Publish Your Purpose Press.

Ordering Information: Quantity sales and special discounts are available on quantity purchases by corporations, associations, and others. For details, contact the publisher at the address above.

Edited by: Heather B. Habelka
Cover design by: Lisa Knight
Headshot by: Tyler Ogburn
Manuscript Strategist: Fern Pessin
Creative Consultant: Aaron Borrelli
Typeset by: Medlar Publishing Solutions Pvt Ltd., India
Printed in the United States of America.

ISBN: 978-1-946384-27-0 (print)
ISBN: 978-1-946384-28-7 (ebook)
Library of Congress Control Number: 2017962243

First edition, March 2018.
The information contained within this book is strictly for informational purposes. The material may include information, products, or services by third parties. As such, the Author and Publisher do not assume responsibility or liability for any third party material or opinions. The publisher is not responsible for websites (or their content) that are not owned by the publisher. Readers are advised to do their own due diligence when it comes to making decisions.

Publish Your Purpose Press works with authors, and aspiring authors, who have a story to tell and a brand to build. Do you have a book idea you would like us to consider publishing? Please visit PublishYourPurposePress.com for more information.

Dear Reader,

I have written this memoir with the assistance of ghostwriters and strategists based on my recollections. The Early Years and The Wonder Years are stories written about my childhood and it is through these lenses I write about what I remember to the best of my ability. When necessary, I relied on the help of friends and family to bring clarity to cloudy or fuzzy memories.

Out of respect, privacy, and anonymity, I have changed the names of most people and several locations, thus enabling me to convey the most authentic experience to the reader. In doing so, I have tried my best to remain fair and respectful to those portrayed herein.

It is through the confidence of living an authentic day-to-day life and successfully winning the battle of addiction that have empowered me with the courage to write *Served in Silence.*

There are people who have come in and out of my life. Some may not feel good about how they are portrayed, so to them I offer a quote by Anne Lamott:

> *"You own everything that happened to you. Tell your stories. If people wanted you to write warmly about them, they should have behaved better."*

Upon completion of reading my memoir, it is my deepest hope you [the reader] learn from my examples, trials, and tribulations of the struggle to live authentically, while also experiencing the successful achievement to that end.

Live authentically,

Dedication

I dedicate Served in Silence to every brave individual
who struggles to live authentically.

I also dedicate this book to my brothers and sisters in arms
in the United States Military who served in silence.

For some that gave all, may we never forget freedom is never free.

Contents

Foreword

Even though I met Mark during one of his darkest periods, when he was "living" in Costa Rica, I remember him as a "get up and go kind of guy," always making others laugh, smile…always authentic and honest…always real with everyone else but himself.

I saw Mark torture himself while holding everyone else up. I watched him slowly killing himself by drinking and not taking care of himself. His family and friends begged me to do something about it. What could I do? Nothing but hold Mark's hand as he walked over these bridges of life, tumbling further and further down the dark pit of nothingness that he was digging all by himself. I believed that Mark knew what was best for Mark.

I remember watching him drag himself in and out of my life: sleeping on my couch, staying in one of my rooms, helping watch my son. Despite his destructive behavior, I always knew I could trust him, and as our friendship deepened, we began to talk about life. About the important stuff. About who we really are and what our real purpose in life is. But I also listened to him tell stories about his life—who he really was on the inside instead of what happened to him. I watched his spirit, his purpose slipping further and further away. And for the first time in my life, I understood unconditional love. I could simply love Mark with no expectations and be his friend no matter what. This was the greatest gift that I have ever been able to give and receive in return.

I remember getting a frantic e-mail from one of Mark's friends informing me he had fallen and shattered his shoulder. It was a blur. See, even during all of this self-destruction and loathing, Mark was never a baby—he took himself to the hospital and got his arm fixed. It was incredible. In spite of himself, his spirit kept him alive.

One night, I e-mailed Mark about an alternative treatment to help him overcome alcoholism. From our deep personal conversations, I knew he wanted to live free from the bondage of alcohol. He accepted this lifeline.

During this alternative treatment program, I watched Mark go from an attractive fellow to very yellow—I mean very yellow, shaking worse than a leaf in a hurricane—fellow. It was horrifying. But Mark hung in there. I gave him my bed and got a mattress and slept on the floor next to his bed. He was so strong and so committed that he carried himself through it! Somewhere, somehow, he got a hold of the real Mark and carried himself through all the pain, the torture, the visions, the detoxing…

But it was worth it. Mark finally understood who he was. He had an open mind and was prepared to do whatever it took. He set aside his confused thinking and discovered the love and joy that he is. He got it! And then, like magic, he began to transform before our eyes! It was more beautiful than a butterfly breaking out of its cocoon. It was more beautiful than birthing a baby. Why? Because Mark created his new reality. Mark clawed and climbed out of the depths of hell and self-torture all by himself. He re-birthed himself while I humbly stood by, cheering and loving him every step of the way.

Mark was physically transformed, his addiction a thing of the past…and now a new world was on the horizon. I watched him discard his past so he could create a new life, a new reality. It was more than taking the bull by the horns; it was watching a god create a new world. It was so spiritually inspiring and so motivating. If he could do it, what could I not do with my life? He showed me what it was like to be fully connected to the world, to others, by being connected to Self, the Self that I call Spirit. Mark became one with life as he learned to truly and unconditionally love himself authentically for the first time.

I am so grateful that he understands *Served in Silence* is not a book about Mark; it is a book about all of us. Mark just had the courage and the commitment to share his silence with the world.

We all have secrets, shame, and horrors in our life. Mark's courage to open up and share this vulnerability with the world is what will change the world.

Mark has touched my spirit and my soul and inspired me to be more courageous than I ever knew possible. And for that I am grateful.

I love you, Mark.
Cheers to living authentically.
—Harmony

Preface

I could not get any reprieve from the war…neither the one outside at Bagram Airfield, in Afghanistan, nor the one in my head. The battle rhythm of the war ground on, days and nights on auto replay. I was physically and emotionally drained, and I was not even to the halfway point of my first deployment in Afghanistan. I was just going through the motions; no choice but to focus on the job that needed to be done. Like ants marching, one by one, back and forth, it doesn't take long to get into the routine of the war—sleeping hut, latrine, office, chow hall, gym. Repeat.

One morning, I looked up toward the snow-capped peaks of the Hindu Kush. The razor edges of the concertina wire sat in giant rolls, like locks of hair, on top of the tall fences on either side of the main road of the camp. How did I get here? Better yet, what the hell am I doing here? These thoughts surfaced while Bryan Adams' song played in my head…"Just a small-town [boy] in the city lights, the best was yet to come. Then lonely days turned to endless nights, the best was yet to come…" I remembered hearing this song as I was leaving for boot camp so many years before.

Bagram, located north of Kabul, was primarily comprised of Army and coalition forces, including the Air Force's Air Expeditionary Wing. I was honored to be the Public Affairs Officer (PAO) for the wing. This particular day, I was preparing for an upcoming visit of dignitaries, and I robotically made my way to the tower in the center of the camp, to advise the air traffic control team of the tour details. I didn't mind actually, because oddly I sought the solace of the tower, as it was a mirror image of what was happening in my own mind—an internal battle of controlled chaos, of good versus evil.

The tower, an old Russian observation tower converted into the air traffic control center, was left standing in Afghanistan during countless years of conflicts and wars. An ugly, fully functional structure of faded, flaking yellow paint, the tower stood as the epicenter, or central nervous system, to bring the full force of the coalition's armed forces to the enemy.

I entered the main doors and started walking up a set of concrete stairs before I arrived at a staircase of stone, with stairs that were smooth and worn. I thought about how many before me had walked these stairs to wear the treads down.

The stairs became narrower the higher I climbed. At the top of the landing there was a metal ladder, like a fire escape on a city building. I reached up, pulled the ladder down, and hoisted myself up the rungs. As I got closer to the opening, I could hear the radio chatter. Once I climbed to the top, I used my head and shoulders to push through the door above me and step into the air traffic control tower, which was a bright octagon-shaped all-glass room. Once inside, I stood upright, nestled up against a "corner" and got my balance. I let my eyes adjust from the dimly lit staircase below.

Instantly, I found myself standing stock still, as I looked to the west to see the sky full of A-10 Warthog attack aircraft coming home from the day's hunt.

The A-10 was an impressive sight with aggressive nose paint and a stellar presentation of air power. The aircraft reminded me of a flying tank with its Gatling gun capable of firing 4,200 rounds per minute. The photos of the aircraft alone were scary, I can only imagine what it looked and sounded like to the enemy on the ground as it flew low and slow, guns a-blazing.

From the tower, the A-10s looked like flies buzzing around as they got into formation to land safely, refuel, and relaunch.

The tower was uncluttered, clean, and with no shortage of air-conditioning for the comfort of the controllers and the protection of the equipment. There was a constant stream of controlled radio chatter that sounded like someone standing in the wind or a vacuum uttering systematic short choppy phrases that a trained ear could decipher. Suddenly there was a sharp distinct warning siren, a sound that rose above the normal chatter to indicate an issue with one of the aircraft in the pattern to land. A plane was coming in "hot."

Everyone remained calm. But I was freaking out. There were old, abandoned minefields on either side and the end of the runway, making an in-flight emergency dangerous. A plane not stopping could be catastrophic! I calmly took a couple steps back to observe. While no one seemed to be overly alarmed, the air and mood shifted instantly in the tower—into one of deliberate, quick, and precise action. Seamlessly and systematically, the controllers pulled the binders off the shelves near their work centers and began running the checklist designed to bring our pilot home safely. The lead controller would holler out the next item and his partner would take whatever action necessary, place a check next to the line item with a black grease pencil, and move to the next item.

As I held my breath and waited for the plane to find a safe landing without setting off any explosions, my mind drifted to another foreign land.

Here I was stationed in the bottom of a great basin, in a country that must have been beautiful at another time in history. The mountains on either side were majestic in nature yet horrifically splashed with blood from many years of conflict. The plains below were no longer lush and vibrant. Now a thick coat of ash from all of the destruction, they surrounded the base and stretched from the tower epicenter until they reached the ancient foothills of the mighty Hindu Kush; its verdant green mountains in stark contrast to the rocky soil below, sown with an endless crop of land mines and strewn with carcasses of old Russian tanks. The base of the mountains formed like great fingers, hopelessly pulling at the edge of the landscape in their feeble attempt to reclaim the land.

I began to daydream about what this plain, basin, and mountains must have looked like as the wrath of Alexander the Great and Genghis Khan plundered these lands. "This place must have been beautiful when it was filled with water and the mountains were lush with green trees and fields of poppy," I thought. But alas, like a toothless old hag, this place had been ravaged by time, the winds of war, and modern-day terrorism.

I felt myself drifting in an almost out-of-body experience, watching as if I were falling into a dark abyss in slow motion, a puppet without strings. Oddly one minute I drifted straight up into the sky. I was suddenly aware that this same bright, pristine sky extended to the world I had left behind. And the sun, now high overhead, while exposing the blemished, blood-stained terrain below in its pure light, shined warm over my home, friends, and family far away. "Ground control, we have a problem. Captain Gibson is experiencing his own "in-flight" emergency. He is shutting down completely—there are emotional land mines everywhere."

The Early Years

Home Sweet? Home

From the foothills of the Hindu Kush in Afghanistan, I traveled in my mind halfway around the world to my home. I was born and raised in the foothills of the Adirondacks of upstate New York, in the Norman Rockwell-like picturesque Village of Ballston Spa.

Ballston Spa, a small, typical American town under an hour north of Albany, is a patriotic place to grow up, with streets adorned with American flags on the houses and lampposts. In the vast valley of the village was the business/commercial district, stores, shopping, municipal buildings, library, and churches, with a scattering of a few houses. At either end of the village, atop the valley's ridges, were the more developed housing areas with beautiful older Victorian-era homes that lined the peaceful streets, steeped with tradition and history. I lived on the south side of the valley in a middle-class neighborhood where the public schools were located.

I grew up in a white house with black shutters on an avenue that bore the name of the village: Ballston Avenue. The house was solid, but drafty. Like objects in your car's mirror, which may appear closer than they seem, such is the case with the house in which I grew up. In my memory, as a child, it was an enormous house. In reality, as each passing year and return visits attest, it was merely the size of a saltbox.

Our house was unpretentious in its décor. It was near-smothering in the sheer volume of knickknacks and bric-a-brac. From the front lawn with ceramic gnomes and a giant green frog, to the inside where every wall was covered with hooked bell-pulls, shelves cluttered with old teacups, and non-functional, broken, chipped, antique furniture that was uncomfortable at best. The "noise" of our stuff was the direct opposite of the "quiet" emotional repression that lived inside.

Remembering my early years is like watching a series of old 8 mm home movies. I was the younger of two boys, only two years apart. At the time, I thought my life was perfect in every way. I had an insatiable sense of curiosity and investigative intrigue—Santa Claus, the Easter Bunny, the Tooth Fairy, holiday rituals, the meals, and celebrations—everything was so elaborate, interesting, and FUN, until we got older and formalized religion entered into the picture. Maybe it was simply that we were getting older and our parents got tired and bored of making the holidays special—I don't know.

Meet the Parents

My parents were kind, caring people, who lived simple lives. My mom was a beautiful former high school prom queen, and my dad was a handsome and debonair, hardworking man. Mom had brown hair, beautiful hazel eyes and stood about 5'4" tall. When she would envelop me into her arms, all was right with the world. Dad, at 5'6", with a chiseled chin, dark hair and piercing blue eyes, was athletically built, with a serious demeanor. He was uncomfortable with displays of affection, and was very imposing, especially when he looked down at me!

My parents were both raised in the country, west of Albany. They grew up among farmers, blue-collar workers, truck drivers, and industrial folk. Vast, rural, upstate New York doesn't get a lot of press as most people hear the words "New York" and immediately think of New York City. My hometown was a world away from the Big Apple.

In my parents' time, life was predictable. Not only because of the era, but because of where, and how, they grew up—isolated and governed by the Catholic lifestyle of hard work and basic pleasures. They were still teenagers when they met, fell in love, got pregnant, and then married (I suspect not exactly the preferred order at the time). Two very attractive, conservative, reserved people bred two very active, handsome, inquisitive boys. They did everything the way they thought they were supposed to, with a hint of providing a better life than the one afforded to them. Yet the basis of their upbringing was the baseline for mine.

The limited media of the 1950s and '60s, also reinforced the scripted nature of my parents' life up to this point: a house with a yard, a mom and dad, 2.5 children and a dog. (We substituted a cat for the half child.) That was our life, and it was simple, mostly happy, and predictable—at first.

Mom was a typical homemaker. A very personable, outgoing lady, she was friendly to strangers and generous to our neighbors—almost to a fault. She had a big heart, was empathetic with a listening ear, and could often be found providing unqualified advice to ease other housewives' marital woes. A decent cook (she loved lots of butter), family-style meals were created in large portions to ensure there would be massive leftovers for the following week. I would grow to loathe leftovers with a passion. It didn't matter if I didn't like what was on the menu for the week. Having it your way was not an option. Money was tight, and we were expected to eat dinner and like it. To voice a culinary opinion at an early age in my house was a sign of disobedience.

"But I don't like onions," the debate would begin.

"Yes, you do! It's all in your head," my parents would respond.

"Yes," I would think to myself, "It is in my head, my mouth, my stomach, my eyes, my nose…I don't like onions!"

To this day, I don't eat leftovers or onions.

My father worked long hours in a tape factory, nearly an hour away, south, toward Albany. He left very early in the morning and didn't get home until late at night. Typically, he was a come home, watch the news, and sit down to dinner kind of guy, with his wife and two little blonde-haired, blue-eyed boys.

Affable and friendly, he was always willing to help others in the neighborhood, and became known for his discretion. He left the gossip and nosiness to the women. Very talented with tools, he liked sports, hunting, fishing, and other manly things, including black coffee and his Winston cigarettes. And while he was not the most affectionate man, neither were his parents or anyone on his side of the family. I remember him as being very strict and stern, preferring to be feared rather than loved.

My brother and I were subject to the discipline norms of the times (which I can safely assume would be considered child abuse by today's standards). There was no such thing as a time-out or the empty promise of, "You're gonna get it." As a mischievous boy, I was always guilty first. The raised voice followed by a stern look was simultaneously followed with harsh beatings with wooden boards, belts, shoes, vacuum hoses…basically anything my parents could get their hands on while holding me down.

Dad's superpowers included single-handedly unbuckling his belt with a Zorro motion striking the floor. A *waa-snap* sound echoed as the leather strap would make positive contact, typically on your backside as you tried to run away. Mom's superpower was the popular Dr. Scholl's wooden flip-flop sandals with a brass metal buckle that could be dual-purposed into a weapon of mass destruction as it was hurled at you and landed on your head or face if you did something she felt was way out of line. Then you had to bring her back her shoe!

A surprise backhand across the face that would draw blood or a fully coiled smack was not uncommon throughout the day. I had a sensitive nose with blood vessels that would burst if I sneezed too hard, so this added dramatic effect to the "discipline."

Mom was strict, but I never doubted that I was loved. It was she who spent the most time with us, as was the societal norm and the case for everyone we knew back then. We fit neatly into the landscape of the puzzle of life, framed by the mores of the times, all the pieces in place, just short of the white picket fence. She managed the house by creating long elaborate lists of chore assignments for the child labor department of the house, "the boys." My older brother questioned this theory one day, "Mom, what are you going to do while I do all of your housework?" I remember the penalty was so great, more than the Dr. Scholl's, that I knew better than to question the legality of child labor in our home.

I don't really remember Mom having lots of friends or being very social outside of the church. I guess that was because her primary role at this time in my life was being a full-time mom. She was very affectionate, often hugging us boys. It seemed to me, by all the attention she gave us, that she loved my brother and me more than she loved herself. We were the primary focus and it appeared she was secondary, last, or not at all recognized. In between the harsh and brutal reprimands and reminders to behave, there were marvelous bonding times filled with an almost magical sense of warmth, love, and wonder.

Despite the harsh discipline, I also recall fondly the days that were filled with the whole family watching *Mutual of Omaha's Wild Kingdom* and *The Wonderful World of Disney* on TV. My brother and I, with Captain, the dog, watched in footed pajamas curled up on blankets on the floor, eating ice cream, while my parents sat on the couch together. My parents did not need a remote control back then, they had me.

Another title I received at an early age was the official eyeglass-finder. "Mark, go find my glasses," would be a normal order barked from the couch. "And don't come back until you do." I am sure this was a novelty at first, almost like a game or activity. After a few years, this request was met with a rolling of the eyes and muttering under my breath, "Why don't you get up and get your own damn glasses?" though never in earshot, as this would surely invoke the Dr. Scholl's boomerang.

Our summer vacation was the highlight of the year. My parents loved the ocean and every year we went to Cape Cod, to the little, quaint town of Dennis, Massachusetts. In preparation for our annual trip, the dining room became the staging area with boxes that would be filled with food, supplies, blankets, suntan lotions, and a collection of travel-size toiletries. The journey seemed like an eternity when I was younger. We would depart at 4 a.m. in order to miss the traffic near Albany. The first glimpse and smell of the ocean air would soon erase the ungodly waking hour and long trip in the car. The water would retreat a great distance during low tide which would expose a vast playground to explore. These were relaxing days of endless play as we stayed on the bay side of the Cape.

Growing up, our family did not have a "keeping up with the Joneses" type of mentality when it came to material things. Instead, we played a psychological game of appearances—where everything has to be picture perfect—especially with the grandparents and in the eyes of the church.

"Don't tell your grandmother, or she will be mad," was a frequent warning.

From an early age, I understood the politics of my life—my family, my relationships, and the church. Say this in order to achieve that; don't be honest because you may hurt someone's feelings or upset someone, and it just went on from there.

Looking back now, I see that at the age of five, this was the beginning of the end for my chance to learn how to live authentically. Such a big word would not befit a young person in my generation. You were given your identity and liked it; it fit within the parameters of societal norms and cult-like religious doctrine and teachings, regardless of what your free-spirited mind thought. It was best, and safest, to keep that to yourself.

As I grew older, I lived two separate lives in my mind. The first was my day-to-day life of doing what was expected, like washing your hands before dinner and brushing teeth before bed; not making any emotional waves by stuffing my feelings down, almost choking on them; and, ultimately accepting a life that looked just like the neighbors'.

Then there was the life I was living in my imagination. In my head, when I was alone, my sexuality was coming into question. This made it hard to know how to act. I explored the emotions of feeling loved but threatened, encouraged but repressed, separate but living in a family of four. In my head, free of constraints, I celebrated, reached high, danced, sang, and spun around until I was dizzy with laughter.

In the midst of this utter confusion, there was the harsh discipline for misbehaving. You may be wondering why the adults at school didn't question the visible evidence of harsh discipline. Well, growing up my mother and us boys attended a black Pentecostal church and around the time I was in middle school, my brother and I were sent to a Baptist Christian school close to our house. Here, similar levels of discipline were encouraged, permitted, and equally endorsed. The religious, Spare the Rod mentality, with parental consent, authorized the school and teachers to execute the same level of beatings on a much more organized, conventional level. And my parents consented.

If I was too mischievous or talked back or asked too many impertinent questions, the teachers would bend me over a metal fold-up chair and order me to keep hold of the seat with both hands. I was whacked on my bottom from behind. Each time I let loose of the chair I'd receive two more whacks from the "enforcer," a thick paddle with holes drilled in it. Between what was happening at home and then at school, I just thought this was normal—that this is how discipline works. As long as my mother demonstrated that she loved me with hugs and kisses, I could deal with the physical pain.

In the full-length mirror behind the door of our bathroom, I would crane my neck to look at my backside, wondering if my badly bruised ass would ever look normal again. The only way I could tolerate it was to disconnect from the reality of my punishments and imagine, in my fantasies, that I lived a colorful, glorious life full of optimistic adventures; and I would make plans for the future, where nobody was forced to eat onions.

I also came to accept the responsibility of my own parenting. Having married when they were barely out of their teen years, they were living like two teenagers in a clubhouse. I knew by the time I was thirteen or fourteen that my parents' emotional growth had been stunted. They had nothing more that I needed.

I was motivated by the desire to never live the life they were trapped in. I vowed to find a way out.

Oh, Brother!

There were times when I idolized my older brother. He was the golden child. He was well behaved at home, which negatively highlighted my high energy and perpetual curiosity. But my big brother adulation quickly diminished as I became the recipient of his harsh words, constant bullying, and physical abuse. He was stronger, afraid of nothing, keenly smart, had a ton of friends, and was a model student—a typical boy that could do just about anything. I was convinced my parents favored him.

During my preteen years, I remember being upset when my friends were more interested in playing with my brother and left me on the sidelines. Sadly, he could have corrected this situation to save me the pain and hurt, but this was another form of acceptable behavior; he was older. He was the perfect kid as far as the neighbors could see. He and my parents related well, yet he and I never really connected.

At home, when my parents weren't around, my brother was brutally mean to me. He would lock me out of the house or tie me up to the telephone pole in my underwear with his friends watching and laughing. He would beat the crap out of me and call me horrible names.

Ironically, as I matured, my outgoing personality, high energy, and natural charisma allowed me to attract friends young and old. My mother and brother would either become threatened or would crave a piece of what I had.

Like many sibling relationships, I suppose my older brother felt that having me, his "annoying" little brother around would cramp his style. He did all he could to chase me away with taunts and physical abuse. Obviously, we did not cultivate a strong, bonded relationship as we aged. Desperate for the fantasy of family and brotherhood, I would minimize my true feelings, toe the line, and cower like a skittish dog waiting to be beaten for something I said wrong.

My closet is where I would often retreat to pour out my secrets to my alter ego; to cry, to vent, and plot my revenge. The closet was my refuge.

Family Ties

From what I understand, life was not easy for either of my parents growing up. We learned from a very young age that when my grandparents visited we were expected to tread lightly, be quiet, and obey. Always obey.

My mother's relationship with her mother, Grandma Vi (short for Violet), was tense, strained, and on the edge.

Mom had grown up in a very small town. Her father passed away while she was a teenager in high school and my grandmother had married several men, giving my mom several half-siblings.

Mom, at a very early age, worked to clean the family truck stop and cabins, and was beaten by her mother for failing the white glove tests.

Grandma was one tough lady who had street smarts and barroom lessons on life, but was not the most book-educated lady. This was often times evident in her choice of language that would send her Fundamentalist Christian daughter into a tirade, "Oh, Mom! Not in front of the children!" This would spark a heated debate that produced more colorful language.

I loved the time I got to spend with Grandma Vi. As harsh as Grandma was to my mother, she showered me with tons of affection and love. Stern when necessary, she never beat me or paid much attention to my imperfections.

My visits with Grandma Vi were special. We did all kinds of things I wasn't allowed to do at home. She let me sit in the front seat of the car, stay up past my bedtime, and I could play cops and robbers in the house (just not in the formal living room). I dreaded when our visits would end. My stomach would be in knots and I would feel sick as I waited for my mother to pick me up. The air in Grandma Vi's home would change, the tension would rise as if a storm was brewing. The inevitable inter-action between my mother and her mother—no matter how brief—was sometimes loud and fierce and inevitably would end with Mom burst-ing into tears. And, although only about an hour away, the ride home seemed like an eternity. With the incessant questioning on the way home, I felt like a soldier who was being debriefed. As a boy, I felt like an operative or covert spy when going over to the other camp—not the enemy, just the "other" camp when I would spend time with Grandma Vi. I would be exhausted by the time we returned home.

My dad's family, the Gibsons, were the opposite of my mom's, at least from a kid's perspective. My father was from a big, Irish farming family. They were meat and potatoes, hardworking folk—definitely not the hugging and loving, touchy-feely type. The children were loved, but love was shown through action—providing clothes, shelter, and food—not through emotion. From what I gathered, it was tough growing up on a farm but my dad's family seemed happy and successful.

Grandma Gibson was prim and proper. She was always very formal and never out of sorts. Her appearance was flawless. She dressed only in skirts or dresses, with every hair in place and very little makeup. She received our visits in the formal parlor. She was stern, cold, and tough as nails. My grandfather, Grandpa Gibson, was the extreme opposite. He was fun and energetic—a roll around in the grass and get dirty kinda guy. He was full of life and funny as all get out.

Ironically, the Gibson grandparents came to every baseball game, birth-day, or special event at school. They supported fund-raisers and school pro-jects. I think we were favored boys, as we were the only grandkids able to carry on the Gibson name at that time.

When my parents met, dated, produced a child, and decided to marry, they merged their two differing family styles, but not their actual families.

Family occasions and visits were separate, for the most part. We would go to my dad's parents' house for a visit in the morning then spend the afternoon with my mom's mom or vice versa. They lived in the same city, walking distance of each other, and yet our visits remained separate, as if they lived on opposite sides of the world! From the outside, it seemed as though they loosely tolerated each other—like they were biting their tongues around us. I was young, not stupid.

For the big family celebrations with my dad's side of the family we went to the home of his sister (who was affectionately called "Aunt Sis"), as my grandparents' place was too small to accommodate the entire brood. This was the stuff that dreams were made of. Celebrating the holidays with my cousins in their ginormous house with a real pine Christmas tree was more magical than *The Wonderful World of Disney*. The Christmas presents would fill the floor space, as each kid had multiple gifts of cool toys and games mixed with practical socks and underwear. It was "the most wonderful time of the year" as the song lyrics would play on the radio and, in my little world, it was my reality. To this day, I love the fall time of year. It's my birthday, the start of the holiday season, and it's packed with fond memories from childhood. Back then it was my time to escape for a brief period…when the day-to-day fantasy world in my head aligned with reality.

Dampened Dreams

I reportedly was developmentally normal during the potty training phase (to which many experts attribute every neurosis). However, from school age on, it seemed that any growth spurts I had were accompanied by such deep and profound episodes of sleep, that they were marked by periodic spells of bed-wetting. Sleep would later become another enemy that I'd do battle with for the rest of my life.

I was starting first grade, meeting new teachers and new children my own age. This was all very stressful and likely the cause of my bed-wetting. But, my bed-wetting was a source of great frustration to my parents, partly because it was something they seemed to take so personally that it would send them into a rage. Rather than trying to help reduce my stress, or find out why I wet the bed, they resorted to yelling and embarrassing me. When blame and degradation didn't produce the desired effect, they resorted to humiliation; ceremoniously draping my urine-soaked linens from my bedroom window, on display for all passers-by to see, including busloads of my school peers.

My dreaded bed-wetting was like a noose around my neck. So much attention and emphasis were placed on it that a gloomy silence overtook me. I began to make my escape plans. I literally felt like I had two personalities. In one personality, 100 percent me, I loved myself unconditionally, it felt like an out-of-body experience. In the world that paid attention to the bed-wetting, I felt broken, like something was wrong with me. The attention created doubt, self-loathing, and hatred of myself. God, how I hated to go to sleep. I was exhausted.

Although I was told that I was not being beaten because of the bed-wetting, but for covering it up, in my mind it was hard to separate the two. It is hard to believe that the words or actions spoken after the fact were the true reason for punishments. I remember being scolded on how to discipline our puppies. I was told they wouldn't remember they peed on the floor and, therefore, it was unfair to punish them after the fact. Hmmm.

When I could bear the beatings and scorn no longer, in desperation, I began hiding the soaked linens in my closet. It didn't take long before my secret became apparent, the air filled with the rancid stench of urine.

Upon discovery, my father beat the living daylights out of me, my mother standing by, watching. When my father wasn't around, my mother would lay on the guilt as thick as any good once-Catholic now-Fundamentalist Born Again Christian could. The extreme was having my nose rubbed in the piss on my sheets, like I was a disobedient dog. Then I'd have to face my brother who would be waiting in the wings to pile on HIS punishment.

I knew I was not an equal member of the family when my brother was allowed to shame me profusely. My dad would often times chime in and repeat his taunts. "Pissy pants" and "piss boy" come to mind. Oddly, these had a reverse effect on my inner self. Small, helpless, I just bottled this up in my plan to show them all I would become somebody.

My parents did not have the tools to deal with my bed-wetting. They blamed me for their feelings of shame, as if I had a choice and was willfully producing urine-soaked linens.

The only one that made me feel okay at this time was Grandma Vi. In her eyes, I was valuable. She never made me feel "less than" and hardly emphasized my periodic bed-wetting. She made me feel special, relaxed, and loved. When I visited, she always made a special spot for me in her bed.

Looking back now, I think it felt special because of the towels and blankets she would put down so that I could sleep. If I had an accident during the night, it was not a big deal. Grandma would efficiently and swiftly remove the soiled bedding, whisking it away as if nothing ever happened.

By the time I was finished with my Honeycomb cereal with bananas (a special treat since it was banned at my own home), I could see the cleaned linens drying on the clothesline that hung from the side of the house to the barn in the back.

This was far different from the public shaming at home.

Halloween Ride

Fall is my favorite time of year. Fall brings Halloween, which ushers in my birth month, followed by the holidays. Halloween in my home was different compared to the homes of my peers in school and the neighborhood kids. Our house struggled with celebrating the holiday for what it was at face value—a commercialized excuse to buy costumes, dress up, and get lots of candy. In our house, enjoying Halloween represented disobeying the newly found, Fundamentalist religion that taught that Halloween was the celebration of the devil's birthday!

That religious stuff may have worked on adults seeking absolution for being "bad," but not on an eight-year-old kid who understood the event simply as dressing up and getting free candy—lots of candy! I suppose I was like any other persistent kid who wanted to get his or her own way. I resorted to bugging the hell out of my parents; especially my mom. I would eventually wear her down to gain access to that free sugar high!

I can clearly remember looking at my mom as if she were from a different planet when she tried to explain how she was told at church that Halloween was evil, and the people that participated in the events were evil. Before she could suggest sitting in a circle in the living room, holding hands and praying, I was off to the next idea of what my costume could be. Even at eight, I knew this evil stuff was absurd kaflooey being spewed in the name of "religion." How could CANDY be evil?!

I imagine it was difficult parenting a kid like me. I did not respond to "because I said so." Even as a young kid I was analytical and observant. I challenged authority, pushed limits, and asked a multitude of questions that would surely wear out the most patient soul.

This one year in particular, when the heat was turned up in the church, threatening hellfire and brimstone, I knew I had my work cut out for me if I was going to go trick-or-treating. One day I noticed a flyer on a telephone pole in the village promoting a Halloween costume party at the fire station on the opposite side of town from where we lived. "Aha!" I folded my hands clasping my fingers together pressing on my chin. This was the ammunition I needed. Certainly, firemen (who my parents taught us to respect and admire), could not be doing the dirty work of the devil? How could Mom make the case that firemen were all evil sinners for hosting a Halloween costume party?

I knew I had to work overtime to get the high hell holy day festivities approved. I got to work on my mother and gently planted the seed, without receiving much of a response. Maybe she was too tired to debate me, I don't know. I then went to work on Dad to enlist his support under the guise of bonding with his youngest boy. At first, I played it like I needed him to help me with a school project to which he agreed enthusiastically. (I could be very persuasive, at least in my mind.) Surprisingly, Halloween was back on the calendar. I counted down days and was excited to attend my first ever Halloween party complete with costume contest.

I learned that other kids in my class were going to the firehouse party and costume contest. Everyone was talking about their costumes and some even had the expensive store-bought ones already in hand. Panic stricken and distressed, I ran home and rushed into the house to alert my parents of this five-alarm emergency. I needed a costume and it had to be great; better than great, it had to be out of this world great! I needed all hands on deck to make this the best costume the Village of Ballston Spa ever saw, in epic proportions. I even solicited and accepted help of the brother.

In my mind, I believed only a store-bought costume would win, because I had seen the pictures of elaborate costumes the school kids would show off in class. Bummed and disappointed that there wasn't money to make this critical purchase, I played along in order to go to the main event. I wasn't happy but I started to rally with the idea I could make the best costume and win the day. I was up for this challenge, because it ensured we were going to celebrate the devil's birthday and I was getting candy!

Under the powerful influence of TV and Walt Disney (*Herbie the Love Bug* was a huge hit at the time), I was convinced that a yellow Herbie costume would allow me to win. "WIN!" I proclaimed dancing around the living room in footed pajamas. I would then hurriedly shuffle up the stairs to my boy cave where the secret drawings of my costume were kept and work on them some more. The entire house was abuzz; everyone in on the development and construction of the costume; even my brother who seldom gave into my childish endeavors being a whole two years older!

Because Dad worked at a tape factory we never had a shortage of tape in our house. You name it, we had it! A peek under the hood or open cupboard doors would reveal tape holding everything together. Silver duct tape, metal tape, black electrical tape, yellow tape, red, all the colors of the rainbow.

I hopped up onto the long wooden bench at our massive country wood dining room table. Typically, I would loathe sitting at or working on this dungeon-of-doom, makeshift classroom table, where my dad would sip black coffee, smoke cigarettes at one end of the table with me in the middle, being grilled with times tables or geography lessons. I was barely tall enough to hold up my head with my elbows on the table. If I didn't answer correctly, I might get a smack on the back of the head, where my chin would then smash into the edge of the table. And I would receive constant and harsh reminders to sit up straight! But for the costume contest, I did not mind this table at all!

I drew up the blueprints for Herbie the wearable car. My legs were not even able to touch the floor, swinging back and forth excitedly on the long wood bench as I sketched and planned. Occasionally, so deep in concentration, I would bang the back of my ankle up against the support beam of the bench; damn that was like hitting your funny bone only on the back of your ankle. Ouch.

Looking back, I am sure Mom loved the idea of me making my own costume, as it kept me busy and out of trouble around the house. I spent what seemed like hours developing the blueprints. I would start by taping blank papers together to cover the entire length and width of the huge dining room table. Dad hooked me up with a solid cardboard tube in which to store my top secret designs.

Creating blueprints was a Dad requirement. Each night, for an entire month, I would wait anxiously to hear that old, green, international truck pull into the drive before running to greet my father at the door with the latest rendition of my General Motors-style perfect blueprint of the wearable, yellow car costume.

Dad could barely get in the door to drop his briefcase before I pounced. Mom would chastise, "Wait for your father to get in the door, Mark." But Dad could sense the urgency and excitement and would quickly follow me into the dining room. I remember his clothes smelled like cigarettes from his long ride home as he would seriously and carefully inspect each line of the blueprints, pausing for effect to inquire, "How do the engine and belts run?" And then we'd burst out in laughter, as I seriously answered, "There is no engine! I am the engine! I am going to wear the car and win!" He'd smile and nod, and say "Okay, go get washed up and we'll review after dinner." I carefully rolled my blueprint and placed it into the tube, and away I would go, scampering up the stairs, almost wiping out as I rounded the corner to grab the banister to pole vault up past the first three stairs.

After my father inspected each draft, I would make the necessary updates following his recommendations. We did this repeatedly until it came time to begin production. Construction of the Love Bug was going to be a major event in our house. Clear the table! Get the tape!

In the end, the finished car did not resemble the blueprints nor a Volkswagen Beetle like Herbie. Instead, it was unique and fun. We took the cut cardboard pieces—the shell of my "car"—outside, spray painted the whole thing bright yellow and assembled the pieces into a "car" using metal tape.

I was not charged with the painting. This was a mom and older brother project. They applied the tape when the painted pieces were all dry as I paced in the front room of the house, hollering out instructions from afar like the foreman. Then Mom finally presented the finished product to me, and it was spectacular in every regard!

From the beginning, my mother was the mastermind of the entire project, ensuring cooperation from my dad, keeping my brother in line, getting me supplies, helping me with the concept, and even working on the car. I was in awe of how we all pulled together to create what was sure to be the winning costume! I just knew it; I could feel it in my bones. I tried it on and practiced my maneuvers, with sound effects and all; it was so very cool. I stood around in the costume for a couple of hours refusing to take it off until my dad got home.

Then the momentous day arrived. Halloween 1977. We loaded up the makeshift Herbie costume into the car and the whole family headed to the Ballston Spa Fire House at the top of the hill, across from the awesome pizza place (Mama's), on the north end of the village.

The neighbors all assembled to cheer me on as the judges called for my age group to assemble. The contestants were asked to walk in a circle in the open bays of the firehouse (the trucks were parked in the driveway), for everyone to see the costumes from all angles. I stood proud and tall to showcase our homemade costume; the one my parents convinced me was way better than store bought. I did have momentary doubts as I looked around at the kids in store-bought costumes, but as we stood there, when the voting was done by applause, I remember how proud I was when they called "Herbie, the yellow-car" as the winner of the costume contest! I won! I won! I looked around in disbelief. I could hear myself laughing and cheering.

I remember trying to ditch the outfit and run to my mom—we did it! I will never forget that feeling of being accepted and equal in my community and family. I think I even shared my candy with my brother.

Later, it occurred to me that while my enthusiasm for this project was definitely the candy, spending time with my family and having my father's input on my costume's construction was no doubt what made the whole process so unforgettable. I was the team leader, chief architect, and developer, and at this particular time in my young life, I did not feel "less than" or not good enough. They were proud of me.

This costume contest was the first time that it was really clear to me that "winning" was the important thing. The idea of getting the recognition and receiving a prize was what pushed and motivated me to work as hard as I could. Winning the contest meant I was valuable. I had worth. I gained attention and recognition from my family, the neighbors, our friends, and my peers. And, maybe I was a little happy to divert all the positive attention away from my brother and have it shine on me for a little while.

The Neckerchief

When I was around ten years old, there was a special announcement made in my homeroom class. It was an invitation to join the Cub Scouts in my community. The teacher made this announcement sound mysterious, special, by invite only, and almost a form of civic obligation. This tactic worked; it gained the boys' attention and created a buzz of excitement. I didn't even know exactly what the Cub Scouts stood for or what they did, but I was excited at the idea of making new friends.

Being a Cub Scout offered another costume to wear. Not only did I love the uniform—the crisp shirt, the cap, and especially the yellow-orange neckerchief and the gold slide that I affixed around my neck—but I did not have to let out the secret that at home I was a bed-wetter and less than my brother. Maybe my parents would be compelled to pay more attention to this different person, a Cub Scout, versus the troublesome bed-wetter. Maybe this new person wouldn't be picked on and bullied by the other kids at school.

Being part of the Cub Scouts would allow me to become a different person.

I don't think I was conscious that the Cub Scouts were trying to teach us values—how to be a good person, help your community, and learn life skills—but that was certainly a secondary benefit.

I liked the Cub Scouts. I liked the camaraderie. I remember going to a local kid's house each week after school. The pack leader was the mom of one of the fellow Cub Scouts. The way to excel was simple: do your lesson and be awarded a badge. Each week, I'd hurry home after classes let out, change into my uniform, and race over to the meetings. Mom would take me sometimes, other times I just ran through the woods behind our house or rode my bicycle.

Compared to today's parenting, I think I had way too much freedom as a kid. I don't remember my parents being around that much. We never locked the door. I just went in and out of the house based on my own schedule. My older brother was home, but he had his own stuff to deal with and I was not a concern. Mom had started doing church work, selling Tupperware, taking on part-time cleaning and retail jobs. I learned to be independent when I was very young.

Soon after I joined Cub Scouts, the first team-building competition was announced—the annual soap box derby! The derby was going to be held at St. Mary's, the local Catholic high school. St. Mary's was affluent—from the architecture of the building, to the uniforms of the students, it was clear to me that only the rich kids got to go there.

The best part about the derby was my dad and me building the soap box car together, being able to spend quality alone time with him. I don't know if this was forced fun on Dad by my nagging mother or it might have been a father-son ritual that he didn't mind. Regardless, it was special.

The soap box derby came and went. My car didn't do very well. But it was a chance to spend time with my dad without competing with my brother for Dad's focus. And although we didn't win, I think Dad was still proud of the fact that I did it.

Cub Scouts quickly became boring. I'd already gone to school, come home, ate a sandwich or snack, changed into the uniform, hurriedly did my list of chores, and then rushed back out. The last thing I wanted to do was sit there for another lesson. I still had homework to do. I had way too much energy that needed to be expended somewhere else! Cub Scouts became a lot of "work" and I started to get in trouble.

What kept me going to the meetings each week was my intrigue with the very clearly set parameters of "if you do this, you get that." In addition to the uniform that I loved to put on, I coveted the badges I earned. It was very cut and dry—if you volunteered in the community, for example, then you'd get your volunteer badge. And the troop, as a whole, had the opportunity to earn badges as a team. That part of it was what I really liked. I belonged. I could achieve.

Captain, Cricket, & Cesar

Going to a scout meeting one day, I learned of a big (I mean BIG, at over twenty pounds) Maine Coon cat that needed to be adopted. I brought the cat home, "Can I have him?" I whined. "I'll take care of him. I'll feed him and give him water," I promised. Surprised, my parents acquiesced, and we took the cat in. I thought to myself, what was one more cat in addition to Cesar the blind-eyed and crocked-tail Siamese cat we already had? He made a really cool sound when he meowed, so I named him Cricket. Cricket turned out to be a great cat that lived with us for a long time.

Cricket was an outdoor cat. Like new toys after the Christmas wrapping is thrown away, my interests became diverted, and I was derelict in my caregiving duties. One day, Cricket just disappeared. We don't know if he gave up on us as his family or if some tragedy befell him. But one day there, next day gone, and I'm not even sure we really noticed for quite some time.

We also had a dog, Captain. He was an outdoor dog. After many years of companionship my mother told me she was going somewhere with the dog and that she needed my help. I got the dog into the car and off we went. She pulled up to the veterinarian's office and told me to take the dog inside.

When I got to the reception desk, the staff told me they were instructed to put the dog down. I was so confused. I was upset. My mother had left me there. I couldn't object or fight, I was paralyzed. To this day, I don't know what was wrong with the dog that he needed to be put to sleep. He was old. Maybe around sixteen years. I wasn't quite that age myself.

Gone too Soon

My home was an emotional minefield—one misstep and the mine blew up. But if you stayed the course, everything was "safe." I realized from a very early age that my parents' abilities to provide a healthy and emotionally balanced life were limited based on their own family dynamics and upbringing. There were no life lessons of dealing with conflict or disappointment. Our emotions and actions were driven by guilt, shame, and secrecy to cover things up or brush them neatly under the rug.

I got agitated about going to Cub Scout meetings because my household "chores" were constantly increasing. The list of chores went far beyond just taking out the trash and cleaning my room. I was tasked with scrubbing floors, washing windows, and cleaning bathrooms. By the time I was in my teens, I was cooking meals, grocery shopping, fixing appliances, and managing the house. No wonder I grew up fast—a childhood gone too soon. I was sixteen, had access to the car, and functioned as an adult running a household.

Of everything I was responsible for, I actually didn't mind the grocery shopping so much. I would put cases of beer on the bottom of the shopping cart and the cashier would ring it up. If questioned, I would just say, my mom ran to the car because she wasn't feeling well—it worked every time!

Male Bonding

By the time I was born, bouncing onto the scene, my parents had barely enough time to deal with their own authenticity. They weren't living their own true lives, and now they were encumbered with kids—one well behaved and one that was quite a handful.

Mom, desperate to see her boys bond with their father, would encourage (nag), my father to include both boys. I would hate it. Especially fishing. To this day, this is something that I don't understand and for which I have zero patience. I had absolutely NO desire to do these forced male bonding activities. I would grow to loathe them as much as I sometimes loathed myself. My brother? He loved it! He was in his glory: he had the lingo down, knew how to bait a hook, and was fluent in the rules of the canoe and fishing. Dad was proud. Me? I was in the way. I rocked the boat.

I was a giant ball of constant energy and sitting quietly was not my strong suit. I remember one time when the three of us were in the canoe. My dad was growing increasingly impatient with me. He scolded me several times to "be quiet," "sit down," and "stop moving around so much or you'll tip the canoe." Sure enough, accidentally (or was it?) I stood up, tipped the canoe over and we all got soaked. Since we lost much of the fishing tackle box and all the bait, boy, was I in trouble! I think secretly I was hoping that was enough to never get invited back again. It worked. Fishing became the dad and brother excursion. Good riddance!

This only increased the gravitational pull for me to become closer to my mother, separate from my father and brother, and to become even more independent. It was true—I admit it—I was a momma's boy. In spite of the guilt, shame and embarrassment of the bed-wetting episodes I had tried to navigate through, I needed to know I was at least favored by one parent. So, like a moth to the flame of her zealous discipline, I was pulled in, looking for the comfort of her random affection.

I loved my dad and no doubt, he loved me. But, like his parents before him, there was not a lot of outward emotion or feelings expressed. Conversations in our house were surface and nonconfrontational—zero drama and zero emotions. If emotions were presented, they were met with stone cold reactions and resistance. I don't think I can count on one hand the number of times I ever saw my parents argue, fuss, or fight. Repression was the name of the game. *Don't ask, don't tell.*

According to *The Brady Bunch* and to my schoolmates, Saturdays were supposed to be spent romping in the woods or riding bikes with friends, but instead, we spent Saturdays getting dirty from driving our garbage bins to the dump.

We lived in a village, but just outside the city limits, so we did not have access to city water or garbage removal services. Instead, we had nifty fifty-five-gallon drums in our back yard that would hold our trash and then, when full and overflowing (with a stench to boot), we would have "male bonding day." All three of us would go to the dump to lift the bins, empty the trash, and wash out the pails. Saturday morning trash days would begin with Dad throwing open our bedroom door, LOUDLY, turning on the overhead lights, and calling us to service! To this day, I swear I will never have overhead lighting in my bedrooms. It brings to mind a most disgusting chore from childhood, not to mention being uncomfortably jolted out of a sound sleep.

It was during these trips to the dump that I would pledge how my own home would be. I pledged that I would never have a kitchen stove elevated on paint cans, or a washer with no dryer, or live in a house that had a septic tank that bubbled over into the backyard for weeks/months into the heat of the summer—disgusting. I pledged that my home would be filled with laughter and warmth, and there would be no corporal punishment. I dreamed of a home filled with plenty of fresh linens, candy whenever I wanted it, celebrations of all holidays, and lavish parties—all in a clutter-free, stylish, and spotless environment.

I think both parents tried to provide a lifestyle that was different, and better than their own, but I don't think either of them had ever experienced authentic living until much later in life. Even today, I don't know for sure.

Taping it Together

Growing up, I felt like my dad didn't know what to say or how to deal with me. My brother effortlessly conformed to the "manly" stuff. I could not sit still long enough to pay attention—but I was innovative and entrepreneurial!

One night at dinner, while talking to Mom about his day, my father mentioned that he was having a difficult time finding a supplier. Basically, he needed to create a bag with a label and serial number to identify the six rolls of tape placed inside it. I offered to do this mundane task. I loved the thought of making money!

I was a natural. And I quickly took the "job" to another level and established my own business with the name MDG Enterprises. I billed my father's company for services rendered via handwritten invoices on notebook paper.

I set up an assembly line which consisted of a broom handle laid over two five-gallon buckets to hold the rolls of labels and the container to hold the bags. I would slap those labels on the bags lickity-split and move on—making a penny per bag/label. I would do hundreds of bags, carton upon carton while listening to music, and later, with money I earned, watching my own black and white television. I had created my first successful entrepreneurial venture!

Here I was at eleven years old, earning money, buying my OWN television, outfitting my own office and designing an assembly line! I thought I was such a big shot! I had matured beyond my parents' capacity to understand me. (If I were this child today, I would have probably ordered my own business cards too!)

My father's project was something that made me finally feel equal in my dad's eyes. I felt like I had recognition from him that was usually reserved for my older brother.

My productivity and ambition were scoffed at by the rest of the family—until I had enough of my own money to buy jeans, Nike sneakers, and the like. Now, my brother wanted in on the gig! So my mom started to take half of my earnings and gave them to my brother! "Sharing and fairness," my mom preached. Fairness? Hell! I would think, "He didn't do any of the work!" So, when I realized that I was actually only making half a penny per bag/label, I closed down that business.

What Would Jesus Do?

The forces that tore this "fairy-tale" American family existence apart were subtle. There was no single event that culminated in the end of our family as we knew it. It was more like the slow sinking of the *Titanic*. Around adolescence, I just felt a slight shift, but it didn't scare us or interrupt our lives, we simply continued to hear the musicians in the background on the deck of the slow sinking vessel of my childhood.

Around the time I started elementary school, at about five years old, my mother became a Fundamentalist Christian, which was no small thing for an Irish-Polish-Lithuanian Catholic girl! We began attending a little, primarily black, Pentecostal church in Saratoga Springs. It was a whole new world. We went from nominally attending services in a lofty Cathedral where robed officials recited mass and incense filled the air, to a little, sunny chapel filled with loud gospel music, where old ladies in big hats spoke in tongues, flailed, and jumped about.

My dad, who was not religious at all, did not fit into this new congregation and this created a terrible strain on their marriage. He refused to attend this highfalutin, whooping and hollering kind of church where being "born again," "saved," and "Christian" were the prerequisites.

In fact, the minister, an older man with a husky voice and piercing eyes, told my mother outright, "Sister Gibson, your husband will never get saved and know the Lord if you continue to come here." He was suggesting that Mom take us kids to a more "appropriate" church that would appeal to her husband, so we could all attend services together.

Somewhere around late elementary or early middle school time, when the church began to dominate my mother's life, my mom somehow convinced my father to open two Christian bookstores. One was an A-frame on a busy highway and the other was in a little strip mall filled with other Fundamentalist vendors. Neither of the stores succeeded. They went bankrupt within a year or two, almost as quickly as they were opened. Their failure was blamed on bad economic times, but it was no doubt a combination of both bad economic times and a lack of retail experience. Regardless, this inflicted a devastating blow to our family, our finances, and created a major crack in their marital foundation.

With countless hours of praying for increased acceptance by someone or something, Mom was focused on getting her entire family together in one church. This would later be the linchpin that was pulled to begin the demise of her family, as she knew it. We tried various churches, each more peculiar than the last, and finally, with Dad in tow, we began attending a small church north of Saratoga Springs. The minister there was a woman. She was dark-haired with sallow skin and darker eyes and she wore an expression that implied that she knew a secret about you (and not necessarily a good one). She was in control of everything while her tall, gawky, cigarette-smoking, cowboy-like husband, stood quietly to the side, in her shadow.

As in many Fundamentalist churches, the congregation fell into a submissive role around the minister. As the anointed one, she was never to be questioned. This was a disaster in the making, as my mother, the Queen Bee of our house, was never to be confronted, challenged, or disobeyed. The slowly forming competition between the minister and my mother for my father's attention would soon get ugly and turn things upside down. Mom did get what she had desperately prayed for, for so many years. Her husband joined her at church, as a family should.

At first my father's response to the female minister seemed to be one of respectful reverent dedication. Their friendship grew and their visits with each other became more frequent. I don't think they ever delved into a physical relationship, but the minister began interfering with our family. Someone obviously let her in.

I think the minister was trying to help mend the cracks in the family unit that two teenage boys (I was around fourteen then) coming into their own, were creating. Mom was losing control. The physical beatings and "discipline" were no longer effectively working on her maturing boys, as we were now taller and larger than she was. Dad didn't really notice much as he was seldom home, consumed with the new church, work, or helping someone with a leaky faucet.

But it wasn't until the minister began walking on the beach at my mother's beloved Cape Cod, arm-in-arm with my father—my mother walking behind them like some dutiful concubine—that people at church outside of our family circle judged us and began to question our role at the church.

My mother was considered a demon-possessed reprobate when she questioned my father and was abruptly slapped across the face by the minister for her lack of submission to them both. This was equivalent to beating a lamb or clubbing a baby seal. My mother carried enough Catholic guilt and was emotionally and physically abused sufficiently in her childhood to make her take full responsibility for this act of treason, of heresy, to dare to question her husband, and worse, her minister!

It was at this point that the little warmth that had filled our home in my early years cooled to an uncomfortable chill. As I entered adolescence my parents were barreling toward their own midlife crises that would change our family forever. Looking back, it almost seemed like someone had turned a switch, and everything I knew before was suddenly changed.

As I came into my own awareness of who I was and what I wanted, I found it difficult to communicate with my family. My desires and curiosities all were shoved into that proverbial closet. After all, sex and sexuality were certainly not acceptable conversation over the five gallons of split pea and onion soup for dinner, especially in the cult of Fundamentalist Christianity that spewed hate like gushing lava on Sunday mornings.

Fags or faggots, the motion of the pinky lifted while drinking tea, and the terms "light in their loafers," were the ways people in the church described the gays. Not really understanding what that all meant, I knew it was not nice and it was reinforced with the vivid descriptions by the cult leader, a.k.a. the minister, on Sundays proclaiming homosexuals would die a thousand deaths while burning alive. Wow, some scary shit for a young man to consider as he's figuring things out. So even then I questioned myself—because that is what Jesus would do, right?

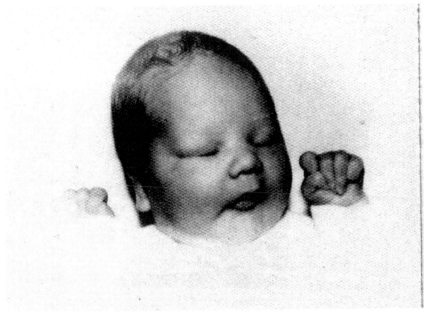

I was born on November 21, 1968.

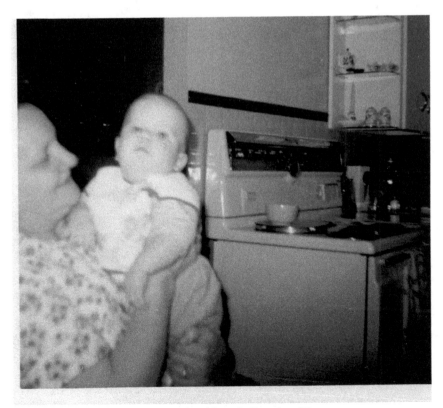

Five months old, with Grandma Vi

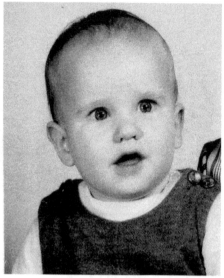

One year old in 1969

With Jet the German Shepherd, circa 1970

The Learning Years

In the Middle

At school I was younger than most kids because I started kindergarten early. Even though I was a cute (so my family told me), blonde-brown-haired, blue-eyed kid, I was short and scrawny. I *might* have been a tad bit precocious as well. I was just curious about everything. Inquisitive—probably to the point of annoyance—if I look back now. That didn't bode well for support from the administration at the school. Furthermore, middle school is where I first experienced being bullied outside of the home.

By the time I began middle school, I was having problems at home. My family did not know how to deal with me. From taunts and teasing by my brother ("pissy pants") that were ignored by my parents and psychological punishment (shoving my face into urine-soaked sheets) for childhood bed-wetting, to verbal abuse for not being interested in sports and athletics like my brother, my life at home vacillated between a stereotypical happy Disney-like home to my own personal hell of being totally misunderstood. I had always hoped being at school would be the best part of my day.

I was a decent student; not a genius, but I did just fine. I would not say that I was a troubled kid or that I hung out with the wrong crowd, but I was mischievous, bored, pushed limits, and found myself in troubling situations.

I think most of this was because of my penchant for challenging authority. I seemed to find myself in the principal's office frequently.

While sitting and waiting for my reprimand and/or punishment, I befriended the front office administrative assistant, Mrs. White. While Mrs. White, a friendly, physically fit woman in her forties, was busy filing, running copies, or stapling packets of information, we chatted. She dressed in classy, upscale clothes and wore designer jewelry. She seemed like she had it together, so when she encouraged me to become involved with student activities to help me be more accepted by my peer group, I decided to give it a try. I joined student council.

One of the duties of the student council was to support the front office by helping new students become acquainted with the school. Offering the tours was scheduled on a rotation basis. My name was next on the list, and I was hoping the new student would be a boy—somebody I could be friends with! My dreams came true as a new Army family moved into town from California and their son entered the school system. I was selected to be the escort for Tommy, newly registered in Ballston Spa Middle School.

Tommy was tall, compared to me at the time, with a stocky football build. He was super nice, polite, and very cool. I knew right away that he would fit into the school without any problem. He was funny, loved talking sports, and was a jock who could play any sport. He played basketball and football and was just an all-around good, simple kid. He was also very well built from lifting weights, which (I didn't know why at the time) I found attractive.

It was quickly evident that Tommy wasn't the smartest kid in the class. This is where I saw an opportunity to step in and help him. Since I was his escort from student council and knew Mrs. White in the front office, I managed to get him in as many of my classes as I could.

Tommy came at a perfect time in my life, I was lonely, separated from my childhood friends, and not very popular. I was getting bullied so often that I would plot the routes I would walk home or buses I would take based on the "safest" route to avoid the bullies. Since Tommy was bigger and stronger, he became a bodyguard of sorts; a bulldog that stopped or minimized the bullying.

Tommy figured out that I was timid and afraid of the other boys. He was not afraid at all. He walked right up to the biggest bully, grabbed him by the throat and said, "If you mess with Mark again, you'll have to deal with me." I remember walking away looking smugly over my shoulder, thinking to myself, "Yeah, take that for all the times you pushed me down and threw dirt in my face or kicked me from behind when I was peeing, so pee went all over my pants. Jerk."

Tommy and I became inseparable at school and then after school. I was around twelve years old at the time. I was definitely at the height of puberty and experiencing all the changes that happen in a boy's maturing body. He was older and more experienced—he'd already gone through puberty and had sex—and he was definitely street-smart. I admired him. Because he was more experienced, I could ask him questions about the changes I was noticing in my own body. He was so comfortable with himself, and I wanted to feel like that.

Tommy and I could talk about A N Y T H I N G. I could ask questions that I couldn't ask my parents or brother. Tommy was mature. After all, he talked about things like tits, masturbating, and sex! Who talks about that in church??? Not anyone I knew!

I would ask questions about my changing body, about girls, about guys. It was no big deal. He didn't laugh at me; he would just talk to me. We'd look at *Playboy, Penthouse* and other girlie magazines, and he'd show me what he'd do when he was aroused. At this point, I knew something was different about me. Tommy was getting aroused looking at the magazines and talking about tits, and I was aroused looking at him getting aroused. He just thought I was the same as him. I was still young when I came to a conscious awareness that I was more interested in a boy than a girl. But that wasn't accepted in my world. It really was not that big of a deal to me, we were having fun and I loved spending time with Tommy.

Tommy could see that I was not very good at sports, or coordinated enough to compete at anything. However, he was always very kind and patient, trying to teach or show me how to play. Sometimes he just gave up and was fine letting me sit on the sidelines and watch him shoot hoops; where

I'd collect the balls for him. I didn't mind because I had a new best friend. He never made me feel "less than." He would change his voice and chatter like a sports announcer as he rolled down the driveway going in to shoot the hoop, and on cue, I would roar like the crowd when he got the basket. He would high five me and bearishly hug me falling into a heap on top of me.

Destiny Re-Imagined

Tommy's family was the polar opposite of what my family had become. I was enamored with his family's way of living. His stepfather was in the Army. His family lived a very regimented existence—at least to the outside world. In Tommy's home, you said "please" and "thank you" and you referred to his parents as sir or ma'am. Wild!

But I liked it; it was comfortable—safe, in an odd, strict kind of way. Tommy did not have the kind of chores I had like scrubbing toilets, floors, doing laundry, or grocery shopping. He was a kid and a kid's kid he was. He played sports, watched TV, and played board games and cops and robbers. It was a whole new world for me. His chores were focused around helping with dishes, taking out trash, and completing his schoolwork. He was helping the family, and he was respected. I always felt like my brother and I were some form of slave labor, but Tommy didn't seem to feel that way at his home. In amazement, he would tell me that my chores were "whacked."

I remember the first time I was invited to stay for dinner when I was at Tommy's house after school, just a few weeks after I first met him. Usually, I would come over for a few hours and then have to leave before Tommy's dad came home.

On this day, as an extension to not wanting our good time to end, Tommy yelled to the kitchen, "Hey, Mom, can Mark stay over for dinner?"

"Fine with me if he gets permission from his parents," his mother, Patricia, replied.

I was so desperate to be allowed to stay. I felt an urgent need to cultivate a friendship with Tommy and staying for dinner with his parents seemed critical. I couldn't risk my mother saying "No!" Without skipping a beat, and without any guilt (I was a kid!), I pretended to call home to ask for permission. I held the button down on the receiver of the phone in the kitchen (I'm not sure what I would have done if the phone rang while I pretended). I made it quick. I nodded my head, and verbally confirmed to Patricia that the phone called produced the optimal result: I could stay for dinner. I rationalized that they wouldn't even miss me at home anyway. And decided that if my parents did figure out that I didn't come home after school, I would deal with the consequences. But this was one opportunity I was NOT going to pass up!

This was very exciting for me. We were just two kids shooting hoops (well Tommy was shooting and I was retrieving the ball out in the yard), and to Tommy, I'm sure it was no big deal. "Boys, your father will be home soon, so both of you get washed up and ready for dinner," his mother yelled to us. This time we truly washed up—hands, face, arms. We stripped down to our underwear to get out of dirty play clothes and changed into pants and shirts. Tommy had to lend me some of his clothes.

I could feel the entire vibe of the house transition, as the head of household, a military officer, was getting closer to arriving home. The blaring rock 'n' roll music was turned down to classical. Then, systematically, Patricia changed clothes into something more conservative, brushed out her curly brown hair, powdered her slightly large nose, and applied simple makeup. The air was charged, and I felt like something big was about to happen. People were PREPARING. Unlike my house, there was no last-minute rush to the table to eat.

I heard the commotion of the dog barking, then the powerful sound of the classic MG Midget sports car pulling up into the driveway and the garage door opening (we didn't have a garage, so I noticed the sounds more distinctly). For some reason, I started to get nervous and Tommy said, "It's okay, Mark; it's just my dad. C'mon."

I could hear his dad greeted at the door by Patricia with the classic "Hi, honey. How was your day?" She then added "Tommy has a friend over from school joining us for dinner."

"Oh?" he questioned. "Okay" he approved.

"Boys, dinner will be ready in ten minutes," Tommy's mom said in a commanding voice, as she cupped her hands like a megaphone from the kitchen to the other end of the house.

I peered shyly into the living room, much like visiting an exotic animal at the zoo when you're not sure what will happen when the animal senses your presence. Tommy's dad had changed out of his uniform and was wearing comfortable, yet casual attire with a collared shirt. Patricia was at the bar cart. I heard *clink* as the ice cubes were dropped into the highball glass and then watched as this was followed by the golden scotch, filled to just the right spot. The glass was handed to Mr. Miller accompanied by a peck on the cheek.

Mr. Miller (I would soon learn his name was Sam, but NEVER called him that to his face), was a tall, lean man, with a handsome chiseled face and blondish brown hair, physically fit and super stiff and regimented, as military men are. He wore gold-colored wire-framed glasses, and chain-smoked cigarettes and, as I learned later, also enjoyed cigars. The smoke would bellow in the form of a funnel cloud toward the reading lamp next to his green high wing back chair as he quickly scanned the paper. While mostly restrained, over time I found that he had his moments where he was fun, within certain boundaries, of course.

Tommy greeted his father and I was led into the living room for Tommy to introduce me as his guest. His father was very cordial and matter-of-fact; deliberate in his tone. He was definitely military, very stern. I can still recall the musical sound of the ice cubes tumbling in Sam's glass as he lifted it for a sip. I was mesmerized by the swirling liquid gold as it cooled around the cubes. Coming from a puritanical Christian home, I marveled at the idea of someone having a cocktail before dinner. I'd entered a foreign land!

"I understand you and Tommy are in the same class at school, Mark?" he asked. This was meant to begin the conversation and for me to explain my role and how it was that I had arrived in his living room.

"Yes, sir." I explained my role in the student council and got a nod of what I hoped was approval. I found Tommy's father to be intriguing. I yearned for his approval—maybe to substitute for the unconditional approval I felt was missing in my home.

I was in awe, watching the family dynamics and the formality of a regular Tuesday evening dinner at the Millers' home. It was not like I was a wild animal; after all, I *had* been to formal dinners in my life. My paternal grandparents lived a very constrained but formal life. On one hand, we had big barbecues with lots of cousins and relatives all playing, eating, and laughing. On special occasions and certain holidays, dinners at my grandparents' home were more formal. However, they just did not occur every night after school with such production!

We all entered into the dining room. I took my lead from watching Tommy. While standing there, Mr. Miller said, directed toward me, "I will learn more about you after we are settled in for dinner." And suddenly, there was almost an agenda for our gathering. Dinners at my home, if we happened to all be home to eat together (which was not always the case), involved grabbing for food from common bowls and communication falling more into grunts, pointing, nods, and groans rather than actual conversation.

Tommy's job was to unplug the phone and settle the dog prior to entering the dining room. We all stood behind our chairs. I had no idea what we were waiting for. Then it occurred to me that Tommy took his lead from his father. We remained standing behind our chairs until Tommy's mother approached the table, and not until she sat down, would Mr. Miller chivalrously place her napkin in her lap, kiss her on the forehead, and instruct us boys to sit after he sat down. What in the world??? (It sounds goofy or stiff but it really wasn't; it was respectful.)

Despite it being a school night during a regular work week, Tommy had on what I considered Sunday best dress clothes. The dinner itself was a masterpiece—VERY different from my home. Often, I found myself home alone and at dinnertime I would typically prepare something simple on the stove (with only two working burners) for myself, such as pasta, soup, or reheated food from another meal or I'd make a sandwich. At Tommy's home, there were proportioned courses! And here, the table featured polished silver, china dishes, water glasses, and cloth napkins. On a TUESDAY!

The menu was exquisite that night, featuring some things I had never heard of or tried before. Patricia made everything herself—no frozen food or store-prepared items appeared on her table. In our house, meals consisted mostly of spaghetti dinners or large casseroles. This was practically a ceremonial affair!

I remember Mr. Miller giving his wife the opportunity to present and describe the masterpiece on the plate, as if he was introducing her on stage for a performance. Patricia described the contents of each plate that was positioned at each place setting. As if describing a Monet or an exquisite sculpture, Patricia offered, "Tonight we have pink Himalayan salt-and-pepper-crusted, grilled lamb chops with a mint jelly, served with roasted asparagus and rice pilaf with slivered almonds." I could not even pronounce half of those things and, with eyes wide to take it all in I wondered what in the world is mint jelly? Over time as Tommy's friend, I came to learn that life was very different in a military officer's home. The day was very regimented. There was no television during the school week. Lights-out came early in the evening. Assigned chores were to be done within a specified timeframe. And schoolwork was the priority. Participation in dinner conversation was mandatory. Like delivering a book report to the class, Tommy answered specific questions and had to provide a report on the day's activities.

In my house, the half-hearted, almost obligatory, "How was school today?" was usually met with, "Boring!" And that would NOT be sufficient in this house! You had to present a new lesson you learned and explain what that taught you. After dinner, the adults retired to the living room to read the newspaper, smoke cigarettes or cigars, and enjoy another scotch with delicate jazz or instrumental music playing softly in the background. We were dismissed to conduct the evening chores of clearing the dinner table and preparing the dishes for Patricia to wash them later, emptying the trash, and taking the dog out, and then I had to bid my friend a good night for there was homework and reading to do. And I had a long bike ride across the valley and it was now after dark.

After helping with the evening chores, I entered the living room, cleared my throat to gain attention, and thanked my hosts for dinner and for an enjoyable time that evening. This was all prompted at the encouragement of Tommy in order to remain in good graces with his parents and solidify future invites. Mr. Miller peered over his wire-rimmed glasses and bid me farewell, while Mrs. Miller smiled with encouragement.

It's Miller Time

School continued on, the seasons changed, and my new friendship with Tommy strengthened. I spent all my free time with him. I was no longer bullied at school and felt the most comfortable I had in years. The darn bed-wetting that plagued my early years had finally subsided and, thanks to Tommy, I didn't have to spend empty hours alone in my room talking to my toys and entertaining myself.

I was reluctant to introduce Tommy to my family. Maybe I just didn't want him to see what I considered to be a mess of a family: very disorganized and unstructured—maybe chaotic in Tommy's eyes. I would do anything to ensure Tommy would remain my friend. I wanted to keep my friendship and relationship with him to myself for as long as possible.

In the past, friends I brought home would find my brother much more interesting than me. My brother would steal my friends away, just because he could, not because he had any particular interest in them. Tommy was fifteen to my thirteen; my brother was around sixteen. It made sense for Tommy and my brother to be friends. My brother was in high school and, because Tommy was held back grades in the past, he was still in middle school with me. Each time my brother stole another friend from me, it would cause me great pain and sorrow and a touch of anger would start to ferment inside me. In my mind, I needed Tommy in order to survive dreaded middle school and couldn't lose him to this unspoken competition with my brother. And thus, another little piece of me would become more distant from my brother.

When I did bring Tommy around to our little white house with black shutters, it was for a brief stopover to change clothes, pick up a bike, and run in and out. Tommy was polite. He would greet my mom, say a quick hello, but before my mother could rope Tommy into a long conversation questioning if he knew Jesus Christ as his lord and savior, I would whisk him away with an urgent "deadline." Always in my thoughts was the jeopardy of Tommy finding my brother more appealing, or fun.

One evening, at dinner with Tommy's family, it came time for Mr. Miller to report on his day. Mr. Miller announced at the table that he was going to be deployed for an extended period of time. I felt like someone silently kicked me in the crotch; I couldn't breathe. I thought this was horrible! How could he leave his family? To be truthful, maybe a tiny part of me was asking, "How could he leave me?" But this was nothing new to this military family. This was just one of many times that Mr. Miller would have to leave his family for military duties.

This was all very foreign to me. I had never been away from my parents for more than maybe a week or weekend at camp or a relative's house. Tommy's dad faded away into the background, gone, into the mysterious and distant Army. I didn't even get a chance to say goodbye.

With military enforcement and rules out of sight, suddenly, unexpectedly, Tommy's home turned into something out of the movie *Animal House*! Gone were sit-down dinners, homemade meals, dressing for anything—this was fraternity living! Meals consisted of pizza, fast food, paper plates, and beer. If you felt like having cereal for dinner or sandwiches, you could. Tommy's mom, in my mind, was like a flower child throwback from the '60s. When the man was gone, with a flip of the switch, Patricia wore braless sundresses and smoked (regular cigarettes and marijuana) while listening to Steely Dan, the Rolling Stones, the Moody Blues, and Led Zeppelin. It was wild. There were few, if any, rules and we basically were allowed to live freely as long as we remained in the house, preferably down in the basement so that she knew we were safe. This was my first introduction to partying.

Just like Tommy, Patricia was open to discussing ANYTHING. If we had questions about masturbation, sex, drugs, girls or boys, she was open to answering them. The more taboo the topic, the more fun it was for her. She hated the traditional role of the Officer's Wife and did not conform well.

At the same time, I was branching out on my own and sneaking (uninvited) into local neighborhood parties that my brother was attending. At one of these parties, it happened— something that would change my life forever. I had my first beer. I was hooked.

Mamma Mia

Patricia was a free-spirited woman who craved attention. She flirted with everyone, touched my arm when she laughed, and rubbed my neck and shoulders from behind while looking over my shoulder. She sat around in shorts and tight (or very loose with no bra) tops. Being around her made me nervous at first, she was so free-spirited. It wasn't bad, it wasn't good. It was just how it was at Tommy's house when his dad was gone.

Patricia told us stories about her days in California (where she lived before New York) where she had tons of gay friends in the service industry, and details about all the parties she attended (and obviously now missed). She answered all my nosy questions and thrived on being the center of attention! I tried not to ask very much so she was tipped off of my intentions. Little did I know, she already knew. Patricia's stories and openness were so contrary to my religiously repressed conversations at home that it was spellbinding; like being pulled into alternate worlds on *Star Trek*.

I was still a bit naïve and felt like Patricia was all about me, but I did recognize that Patricia was the same way with all young people who came to the house. We had another military friend who would hang around with us. He got treated the same way I did. She had a mantra: "If it feels good, do it. If it doesn't feel good, do it until it does." Why wouldn't we want to hang around her?

As I compared Tommy's house of freedom with my home, I came to appreciate that people can be many different things. I watched Patricia turn on and off her different personalities based on who was present in the house. I watched my parents turn on their different personalities based on whether they were in church, with neighbors, or visiting family.

One night I told Tommy and Patricia that I needed to leave because I had to get to the store before it closed. "Why?" asked Patricia. "I have to pick up milk for the house," I said. Patricia started to fire questions about why I was the one shopping for the family. She decided she needed to meet my mother. Oh Lord! I did my best to avoid this for as long as possible, but when Patricia came to pick me up to take Tommy and me to the movies, my mother was home. And then it happened. My mother, the Fundamentalist, met the free-spirited flower child hippie.

Patricia told me afterward that my mom seemed like a very nice woman, but she now understood what kind of life I led at home. The good news was that my mother was okay with me spending time at their house and, eventually, she allowed me to go on vacation with Tommy's family.

But the bad news was that weeks after the first meeting, I came home and found my mother and Patricia sitting in the living room together. Much to my horror, and disgust, Mom and Patricia had started a friendship. The Bible was open on the coffee table in front of them, and my mother was teaching! I wanted to die! My worlds were colliding.

I Owe You

I was invited on a family ski vacation by Mr. Miller. I worked my butt off to earn money (mowing lawns, shoveling snow, helping with neighbors' chores, and working odd jobs) in order to join the Millers on their trip. When I couldn't come up with all the money and dejectedly told Mr. Miller I could not afford to go, he paused for a few minutes while sipping his scotch, then told me that he would lend me the money. We wrote out a payment plan where I could pay back all the money at a steady weekly rate. He and I signed the IOU. It was my first contract.

After the trip, I doubled my efforts to make sure I could pay Mr. Miller back early, and I beamed as I handed Mr. Miller the final payment. I was so proud to accomplish my goal. He totally shocked me when he said, "I am proud of you and appreciate your efforts to pay me back early." Then he said I should keep the money and save it for something in the future. He signed the IOU note "Paid in Full." WOW!

On the trip, I relished the way Tommy's dad included me and made me feel special. The resort, in Stowe, Vermont, was like something out of a Hollywood movie—like the Von Trapp home in *The Sound of Music*. There were formal dinners and busy days of snow-related activities. I did not take being included for granted nor did I disrespect Mr. Miller's requests and direction. He took time with me, teaching me how to downhill ski. He was patient and kind and focused on teaching life lessons along with skills. It was never about being less than or better than; Mr. Miller taught me how to find my own strengths and to develop each one.

I felt validated and lifted up when I was with the Miller family; unlike the feelings of being invisible when spending time with my own family. I contrasted Mr. Miller's patient tutelage against the time of me trying to fish with my dad.

And I learned that there were certain things that one could tell this momentary dad and there were other things we were not to talk about in front of the Army Major. Navigating through who can know what and what was forbidden was a familiar routine at my house, so I was right at home. If you aren't asked, you don't tell.

Days of Our (Secret) Lives

After my first sip of beer, I was on a mission; I was obsessed with finding opportunities and ways to get beer. Around the same time, *Penthouse* and *Playboy* magazines were being traded amongst friends and boys at school. My brother had a secret hidden stash of dirty magazines and I would share them with Tommy.

Tommy's house was like a rotating theater in the round: you stayed in one place but the scenery was changing depending upon who was at home. When the military dad was present, there was a military spouse, proper military children, formal meals, and lots of routines to maintain. When the military influence left the home, there was the free-wheeling, free-spirited mother and it was "anything goes" kind of mentality. Oddly, I found it easy to assimilate into each scene as necessary, like changing costumes to become a different character in a play.

When the adults were not paying attention, the influence of the dirty magazines, the beer I was able to find, fueled with raging hormones, led to Tommy and me experimenting, "How does it feel when you do this? Have you ever tried this?" And boy trash talk escalated as we looked at naked women in magazines—trying to outdo each other with what we would do if that woman was in the room with us right now. But I knew in my heart, it wasn't the women I wanted. I wanted the boy sitting next to me. I was aroused by him, not the glossy images in the magazines. Like bed-wetting was as a child, and my recent alcohol consumption, smoking, and my experiments, my feelings for Tommy were just another branch of my secret life that I had to protect.

I can't imagine what would have happened if my parents knew about what was going on at Tommy's home and the secret layers of my double life. At the end of each visit to Tommy's, I was going home to an inhibited family, and would have to walk through an emotional minefield just getting through each day. Ever present was the burden of the secrets I had pushed into my closet and the fear of being exposed. Would my parents find my alcohol? The cigarettes and pot? The magazines? Would my parents figure out I was gay? Would they learn about the partying and sex talk and very non-Fundamentalist Christian activities I engaged in out and about or at the Millers' house? For a developing young man, this was hugely stressful, which just led me to find solace in the bottle, where I could forget and be carefree, laughing away all my issues and dangerously dancing with the devil.

I discovered that I could swim in between the lanes and navigate the changing spaces at Tommy's home with great ease. Most likely it was easy because of all the practice I had living with secrets, shame, and guilt on the other side of the Valley in my own home. Maybe it was also because Patricia, I later found out, knew I was gay. She never said anything to me. She never told Tommy. Perhaps that's why I felt so connected to her.

Fast Times at Ballston Spa High

Tommy and I graduated from middle school. Moving on to high school was a difficult time for me. Partly because of the awkwardness of all the experimenting Tommy and I did during puberty and partly because I was starting high school at thirteen years old. I was awkward compared to other students. I was starting all over again, but Tommy had been teaching me how to stand up for myself. Now, having gone through puberty, I felt better prepared to do so—even when the taunts and barbs about my sexuality were thrown at me like spears as I walked through the halls between classes, or in the cafeteria, or during PE classes.

At the end of my sophomore year in high school (I was fourteen years old), Tommy's father received orders to transfer to Fort Bragg, North Carolina. Being from California, the Miller family was not fond of the brutal winters and snow in the Northeast. The novelty wore off quickly, so this was a happy change for them. But I was devastated! Not only did I have a massive crush on Tommy—he was my entire world, my safety net, and my social life—but I had grown to love the lifestyle and secret rendezvous with Tommy and his family. I could not bear thinking about how I would go back to high school without him in my corner.

Tommy was my beard, if you will: a shield that buffered the extreme bullying I experienced. Tommy was popular, handsome, and built very strong. I always felt safe knowing Tommy was around. Yes, admittedly he was a crutch. And while one might hope that my older brother would have been there for me, protecting me from bullies, he did not. In fact, if anything, he would encourage and join in on the taunting.

Before Tommy left, we dated two girls who were best friends. Tommy's girl was tall and blonde, a real knockout. Her makeup was always flawless and she dressed beautifully. She lived in the middle-class section of town in a nice home. She had money from an insurance policy on her dad who passed away young, but she never flaunted it. She was not only easy on the eyes, she was extremely smart, very articulate, and well connected in school and the community. She came from a single-parent home and her mother worked for the school district.

My girlfriend was a fiery Italian! She had dramatic long, silky, black hair, smooth olive-toned skin, and she was very thin. She was also put together well with designer clothing and simple, natural makeup. She was in all the accelerated classes and in the National Honor Society.

The girls liked to drink wine coolers, always protecting their lipstick by using straws. The girls didn't like smoking, so Tommy needed to smoke his weed when they weren't around.

Since the girls were in the same classes ahead of us, they could give us clues to what certain teachers would have on tests, and what kinds of things to focus on for studying. They didn't tutor us, but they sure helped us navigate through our classes.

Tommy and I would take them out on double dates. We'd go out to eat, to the movies, bowling, and to play miniature golf. We'd park or go somewhere to make out for a long time. Later, after we were all together for many months, we'd rent hotel rooms. We were with them for about a year or so before Tommy left.

Moving On

hile I was busy double dating with Tommy, I was also planning for my life without him by secretly visiting a military recruiting office in the next city over. I learned that I could not join the military until I was seventeen and, even then, I would need a parent's authorization.

Before the Millers actually packed up their house, loaded the truck, and moved down South, my mother, who had become friends with Mrs. Miller, went with Patricia to North Carolina to scout out a new home, get Tommy registered in a new school, and finish up all of the other details it takes to move an entire household. I was not happy about this trip. Just like my brother who would try and steal my friends away, Patricia would become better friends with my mom. And once again, I would be left on the outside, looking in. Mom returned home to upstate New York with stories and descriptive pictures of the houses that they looked at until Patricia settled on the one that they would move into. Later seeing the pictures, I thought—my God, it was a mini mansion.

Once my refuge family moved at the end of my sophomore school year, I kept in touch through telephone conversations with Tommy and Patricia. But telephone conversations could not alleviate the anticipation of the physical and verbal abuse I was dreading when the school year would start. My mind was obsessed with these thoughts. I became more sad, depressed, and anxious with each new day getting closer to the beginning of a new school year.

Without realizing it consciously, I had put all of my focus and attention on Tommy for the past few years and I lost ties with my childhood friends. As I was now larger in size and Tommy had taught me to defend myself, the physical abuse had pretty much come to an end, but the psychological and emotional bullying from other kids intensified. How did they know before I knew that I was, indeed, the derogatory word they were calling me—a faggot? While I didn't exactly know what that word meant, I knew it wasn't a compliment.

Though I no longer was with my girlfriend after Tommy left, both girls remained friends with me and helped me get by for the rest of high school. Being with them gave me a pass based on association. The bullies didn't want to mess with the most popular girls in school.

Sex, Drugs, & Rock 'n' Roll

When the Major deployed and left Patricia to handle the move to Fayetteville, North Carolina, she went through a big depression since it was very stressful. She was having trouble managing Tommy. She turned to my mom. And Mom introduced her to religion.

Eventually, before they moved down South, my mother and Patricia became good friends and Patricia began attending religious services with my mother. They became church buddies. However, *Animal House*-style partying was still going on, so long as we didn't tell my mom. MORE secrets to keep. I didn't care, as long as what I had grown accustomed to didn't change. I just didn't understand why Patricia was covering everything up as much since she wasn't the type to care what other people thought. It all seemed so disingenuous, so inauthentic.

I had a hard time understanding how my "live free" surrogate mother was now coming to church and praying for answers to her problems. I figured it must be because she was acting as a single mom, with a wild-ass teenage son. (What did she expect?) My mother, for some incomprehensible reason, actually thought she could offer some marital counseling (Hello, Mom—look at your own marriage!), and now in addition to my brother stealing my friends away, my mother was stealing away my friend/mom-by-proxy. My mother was encroaching on my world way too much! I never again invited Tommy to come to my house.

When Tommy invited me to visit him in North Carolina for the summer, I somehow convinced my parents to drive me to his new home and drop me off for a long visit. It was a very long drive and I remember we didn't have money to stop at a hotel so my dad insisted on driving straight through. Every hour—it didn't matter if I was asleep in the back or not—he would crank up the volume and we would sing along to Willie Nelson's "Seven Spanish Angels". Every hour. Ugghh.

The house was huge and had a pool. It was in a neighborhood of ginormous homes with pools and tennis courts. This was better than summer camp! My parents stayed at Tommy's house for a few days and then they left to go back up North. "Good riddance, let the party begin!" I was thinking selfishly. The Major was still deployed and would be for the rest of the summer.

It was wonderful to reconnect with Tommy and be introduced to his new neighborhood pals as his friend from New York. It was the summer of sex, drugs, and rock 'n' roll, smoking pot, and pool parties. I slept in Tommy's room. Sometimes on the floor. Sometimes in Tommy's bed. A time or two passed out on the pool furniture. The summer was as wild as *Fast Times at Ridgemont High*.

Migratory Bird

I know that my relentless pursuit of excellence, my need to be liked and to feel approval, and my own embarrassment and shame of things that happened in childhood were forever emblazoned and looming in my mind. This made it difficult to just relax and be a boy. I had to excel. I had to be the best. I matured quickly. Being around Tommy and away from my parents made me realize that I had to figure out a way to be on my own.

Lack of sleep taunted me as it was burned into my mind and memory that bad things happen when you awake with the sheer panic and sickness that you'll get beaten again for peeing the bed. I didn't know how to bring my true self to the family dynamic. Not to mine nor to Tommy's. I was acting all the time; figuring out the role everyone else needed me to play at any moment.

I surmised from observing others around me that there was something different about me. My relationships with friends, family, and people coming into my life was never as easy as it seemed to be for others.

My internal time clock was set like a migratory bird's. I felt compelled to leave home, fly away somewhere else, and achieve something—though what that was to be, I did not know. I was driven by the desire to never live a trapped life. I had to find a way out.

Escape Goat

I devised an elaborate plan to combine two years of schooling into one and graduate early. I convinced my father to let me graduate at sixteen years old by pursuing this plan. If Tommy wasn't here to hang out with, why not keep busy for a bigger goal and double up on the schoolwork?

During this time, I also worked and kept myself busy. I was saving money for a car while working at McDonald's nights and weekends, and selling caffeine pills (a.k.a. speed), sticks of gum, and cigarettes at school, while simultaneously filling the role as President of the Future Business Leaders of America. My double life continued on at high acceleration. The overachiever in me was in hyper-drive with a hint of Ferris Bueller tenacity.

The bullying would come in spurts, but not nearly as often as it used to. I'm not sure if that was because I was growing, because of my friendship with two popular girls, or if I just had a little crazy in my eyes that warned: Do NOT mess with me!

Outta Here!

The weekend after my high school graduation there was a Phil Collins concert at the Saratoga Performing Arts Center (SPAC) outdoor concert venue. I was once banned from going to SPAC for a concert a few years earlier, when Mom was on her church-driven "secular music is for the devil" kick. I missed Journey's Frontiers tour because of that damn devil. And I'm still bitter about it, "What did hell and the devil have to do with Journey and Steve Perry?"

Attending the Phil Collins concert was to be a sort of going away party for me. This time I learned not to ask for permission, but to beg for forgiveness. But it didn't really matter, I was sixteen years old, with money in my pocket, a high school diploma, and my Dodge Omni to hit the open highway to spend my summer in North Carolina. I was told by the recruiter that I couldn't join the military until my seventeenth birthday, so why not spend the summer partying with my best friend? What could possibly go wrong?

The next day, hungover and feeling like crap, I packed up my black (with red accents inside), little Dodge Omni and headed south.

The previous year, my parents and I had driven to North Carolina so naturally, in my teenage brain, I knew how to get from New York to North Carolina—or so I thought.

I remember leaving Albany and looking at the city in my rearview mirror as I was heading south, smirking with confidence. But then I was suddenly nervous and afraid as I remembered my dad had a difficult time navigating the drive through New York City. Albany is a big city, but NYC is THE city! Stories about congestion, traffic, danger, and highway confusion started to worry me. As I got closer to the city, I found the stories were true and my memories were real! What the hell… the traffic picked up and it seemed that everybody drove faster. I was reluctant at first, but held on tight for dear life, pushed the pedal to the metal, turned up the tunes, and made it through the city into New Jersey! I soon found my way to I-95 South. After that, it was pretty much a breeze getting to North Carolina. (Google Maps certainly would have been a welcome companion on that trip!)

For my trip, I had packed essentials for a teenager traveling on an adventure: several homemade music tapes with songs from Journey, Air Supply, Bob Seger, and Barry Manilow to name a few, snacks, and (maybe not so conventionally) a few pounds of marijuana. My plan was to sell the weed once I arrived in order to collect some spending cash. As if driving with a load of illegal marijuana wasn't nerve-racking enough, I was more concerned with having to stop at a hotel on I-95 and pay for a room that totally wasn't in my budget (that apple didn't fall from the tree). Plus, I didn't want my vehicle sitting in a parking lot that could be stolen, broken into, or searched by the police. But at least I did pack the stuff under the spare tire in the wheel well of the car under the carpeted cardboard decking…no one would ever think to look there, now would they?

Risky Business

The reunion in North Carolina was like *Animal House, Part II*, the partying was still alive and well. This time, more comfortable in my skin and feeling like a big shot, I knew what role to play, right down to what clothes to wear. I was cool. However, this house was far grander than the little ranch home on Willow Stream Lane in upstate New York. This was a three-story, traditional Victorian colonial with an in-ground swimming pool in the back. Frankly, I felt like I had arrived at a resort! There were high school and college-age kids always around. Everyone nicely dressed and I was welcomed into the fold with open arms. It felt good and I looked good in my Izod and Polo shirts (collars popped up naturally) and golf shorts.

Tommy and Patricia had a room set up for me over the garage. It was comfortable with a bed, dresser, television, and a chair. But it was hot as hell being over the garage. I had fans and a window air-conditioning unit that I ran all the time. Which was okay with me; the white noise was peaceful and it kept the room nice and cool.

Upon my arrival, I secured my product in Tommy's house, and we began developing our marketing strategy to move the couple pounds of marijuana. The news spread like wildfire and within a few days, the store was empty. I was still only sixteen, but I had made enough cash to sustain me for the rest of the summer. It's no wonder why *Ferris Bueller's Day Off* resonated with me so well as I donned mirrored sunglasses while lying by the pool drinking sweet tea. If this were a movie playing in my head it was *Ferris Bueller* meets *Risky Business.*

The summer flew by and I found myself running low on funds. My car needed to be fixed and the only thing I knew how to do was to get a job and make some money. I answered an ad in the classifieds for a sales position at a major import/export company. Patricia let me borrow a tie and shirt from Mr. Miller's closet, I got into my clunking Dodge Omni, and made it to the interview.

The interview was in a makeshift office, which was essentially a smaller, shabbily built, room located within a very large warehouse. The people I met were extremely friendly, cordial, and encouraging. I have no idea how they believed my fake ID from New York that stated I was much older than I really was, other than to say I was very convincing. Nonetheless, I got the job. It did not pay much, as it was commission based, but it didn't seem that I had a lot of options.

At this time, Tommy was supposed to be going to summer school to get caught up from his crappy grades the previous year. I told him I would help him; he just needed to go to school and focus. I was up early, every morning, heading to work, all grown up at the ripe age of sixteen. Tommy's job was to go to summer school. After fulfilling our daytime duties, we would meet back at the house and plan elaborate weekend parties or weeknight adventures.

It was no surprise that Tommy did not hold up his end of the bargain— he slept in and skipped school (a clever habit he had mastered in New York). He eventually flunked out of summer school. "How the hell can someone flunk out of summer school?" I asked him. I could see he was a disappointment to his mother and I was certain that when the Major returned home, it would not be a pleasant experience. Sadly, this brought our relationship to a fork in the road.

Within a short amount of time, I got a promotion at work. I went from a sales and customer service representative to an account manager dealing directly with representatives from customers. I had no clue what I was doing. I was successful in part because I was energetic and fun on the phone. Again, I was scratching my head thinking, "Seriously, people! You don't know that I'm only sixteen?" I went along cultivating the lie, and the money started to get better.

Things were heating up back at the Animal House, and I knew my time was limited there. My mother's phone calls became increasingly irritable with open-ended questions that I refused to answer.

"When are you coming home?" she'd ask.

"Soon," I would reply.

And here I was yet again, cultivating an environment of secrets—selling pot and anything else to make money, partying with Tommy, exploring my sexuality, working at a job where I had to lie about my age and background, not telling my mother the truth about coming home, nobody knowing about my military goals—the list went on and on.

"Who AM I?" I wondered every night when I drifted off to sleep.

As Mom's frustration grew, since she was not getting the appropriate response out of Patricia to force me to make a decision, Mom plotted her course of action. She planned to have a strong talking-to with the Major when he returned home. Looking back, it's almost as if she had a crystal ball and could see trouble ahead.

The Jig is Up

Tommy and I ended up getting into trouble that summer. Picking up the same routine we followed in high school in New York, it was normal for us to drop off the girls we were dating and then go out together. This one particular night we were in Tommy's parents' car, just a few blocks from the Millers' house in this very upscale neighborhood, when we decided it would be a good idea to roll a fat one and smoke the joint before going home for the night. (At an early age, pot did nothing for me so I really "did not inhale"—way before a future president coined that phrase.)

I imagine now that the car must have looked similar to Spicoli's car in *Fast Times at Ridgemont High*. You remember the very famous scene of Spicoli smoking so much dope that when the police officer arrives, knocks at his driver side window, and Spicoli rolls down the window, an immense plume of smoke was released into the cop's face? At least, in my mind, when the police officers pulled up behind us and asked Tommy for his license and registration, this must have been what the cops saw.

We could see Tommy's house from the police intervention! This police officer was a caricature of officers depicted in hundreds of coming-of-age movies where the tough cop is going to show us rich kids a lesson. He arrested us. The police impounded the car versus leaving it on the street. It would cost big bucks to get the car out of impound—a lesson to our "rich" parents.

While handcuffed in the back seat of the police cruiser, I was preoccupied, thinking about what a mess we had gotten ourselves into. The police officers decided it would be funny to do a face and neck check by slamming on the brakes. This unforeseen action forced our faces to smash into the bulletproof safety glass between the front and back seats. Ha ha ha—not so funny. THIS was a BIG mistake for them!

Ever since I was a child, my nose was very sensitive. I could get a bloody nose by simply turning my head too fast. Smashing my face up against the bulletproof safety class induced a powerfully bloody nose! I amped it up as a victim like nobody's business.

Even Tommy was getting a little nervous in the back seat as blood gushed from the center of my face, down the front of my white T-shirt, and all over my skimpy shorts. (All I had on was shorts and a T-shirt; no underwear, and flip-flops. This should have given the cops enough information to know we were not planning to go very far; we were not out joyriding!)

The officer in the passenger seat glanced back and noticed I had started to bleed profusely from my face. The two officers got extremely nervous. They knew they were busted for roughing up a couple of boys for simply smoking a joint. The police officer was constantly asking me questions, challenging my age (this time it was trying to see if I was older than I actually was). Once in the police station, I was finally able to prove I was only sixteen.

The desk sergeant came over and yelled at the arresting officer since I was a minor. The sergeant hoped to hell I was not going to sue the department for the physical abuse. Tommy was two years older than me, and he was in fact arrested and arraigned for possession. The officers quickly whisked me off to the local juvenile detention center, where I was encouraged to call an adult to retrieve me.

I frantically began to try to reach Patricia. I was being accosted with a sensory nightmare. The juvenile hall was filthy. The kids in the holding cell with me were definitely in what I considered the "hoodlum" category, rough and proud. (I would not last very long, I thought.) Not to mention that the refrigerator and freezer had apparently broken down, so all of the food had begun to spoil, and the place reeked of rancid meat.

Patricia would not pick up the phone at her house. Patricia loved her scotch and loud music. The soundtrack for my life at the time matched my current age, "Edge of Seventeen" on the *Bella Donna* album by Stevie Nicks. Patricia would blast it so loud that it would echo off the neighborhood houses! That song let us know Patricia was home, and the red light to *Animal House* was on. I knew she was thoroughly enjoying the wild party that had been in progress when Tommy and I left to take the girls home, before we stopped to smoke a joint before returning to the party.

The warden at the juvenile hall was pressuring me to reach an adult, so he would not have to process all the paperwork for an overnight stay. In my head I said, "Oh don't worry, Mister, I am not freakin' staying here tonight." I continued to frantically dial Patricia's home phone, hoping that in the pause between songs on the record, she would hear the phone. Finally! One of the partiers picked up the receiver and quickly just hung up. I could totally see how the phone ringing would interrupt the vibe. Dammit.

Frustrated and scared out of my mind, I continued to call until finally Patricia answered the phone. It took me a minute to explain to her what had happened. She was so confused as she thought we were just upstairs in the bedroom! She had no idea we had even left the house let alone got arrested or abused by the police. "Okay, Mark. Okay. I will come pick you up; give me the address," she sighed in frustration. I gave her the address and phone number and begged her to hurry.

I went back to the day room, which was kind of like a holding room. I covered my nose with my crusty bloodstained T-shirt. The warden came in, and told me I had a phone call. I looked just as shocked as he did. I must have been a terrifying sight to the other kids there, maybe that was why they left me alone—sort of like I looked so bad, "you should see the other kid!"

I picked up the phone and cautiously said, "H e l l o?" It was Patricia.

"What the hell is wrong with you boys? How the hell do you expect me to come pick you up if you got the car impounded?! For all I care you both can stay put where you are for the night!" She was furious! Maybe more disappointed in us, because we were permitted to do *anything* we wanted to at the Animal House; why did we leave there, out of her safety net?

"I won't make it through the night at the juvenile hall!" I pleaded with as much passion as I could, "Please, Patricia! Please come and get me! Hurry!"

She slammed down the phone.

I had no idea if she was going to come pick me up. Shortly after I hung up, I heard a commotion in the hallway

"WHERE THE #$%! IS HE?" Patricia was standing there to retrieve me red-faced and all, for I knew for certain this was blowing her high big time—which was not cool. She signed me out of juvenile hell.

It was quiet and uncomfortable on the car ride home. Patricia was seldom serious.

"Where the heck did this car come from? Whose car is this?" I absently wondered aloud.

"Don't worry about it," she snapped back. When we arrived home, I realized she had borrowed a neighbor's car.

When I was safely back on familiar ground, I began arguing with Patricia about Tommy. She looked at me sternly and said, "The only reason I got you is because you're not my kid! Tommy can sit his ass in jail until I figure out how to get my car back." I agreed that we needed to get Patricia's car back. I was thinking that my keys to the Dodge Omni were on the floor in the backseat of her car! So that rendered two cars unavailable for her use.

A couple of days later Patricia finally thought the lesson was taught and went to retrieve Tommy out of the county jail. When Tommy got home, Patricia sat us both down and told us this was not going to be pretty when the Major returned home in a few weeks. She said, "Mark, your mother has been calling daily and you need to figure out what you're going to tell her."

When the Major came home he was informed by Army officials that his kids were involved in criminal activity while he was deployed. Oh, to say this did not go over well would be a massive understatement! We would also learn he was up for a promotion to lieutenant colonel soon and we felt horrible that this could blemish his record.

I was nervous to be called into the formal dining room, to sit at the judgment table, while the Major interrogated us. It was like the dumb and dumber show where Tommy was silent, following my lead. I was the talker.

His father was reasonable as we talked through everything. He was stern and angry. He levied punishments to Tommy, but he informed me that it was time for me to go. Banishment! Ouch.

This whole incident was devastating. I respected this man. He inspired me. He had done so much for me and had improved my self-esteem. I was embarrassed to have disappointed him. I look back now and realize that I was overcome with nerves because we never confronted anything in my house. Emotions were repressed and we never acknowledged that anything was wrong. My proxy father put everything on the table and I was expected to account for my actions. "How do you do that?" I remember thinking.

Tommy's dad told me that he had spoken to my mother and he encouraged me to go back home to New York. I agreed. Well, kind of. I agreed to leave and they assumed it was to go back to New York. But what they did not know was that the plans were in motion for Raleigh, North Carolina, not Albany, New York. Hoo boy! More secrets. More deception. More time to shield myself from my family. I was on this mission to achieve great things and determined, in my mind, that I would not go home until I was a colossal success!

The next morning, I bid farewell to Tommy and Patricia. I thanked them for their hospitality over the summer and apologized to the Major for getting into trouble. He warned me to stay out of trouble, and Patricia said to call them when I got back to New York as she waved from the front door.

I was handling my shit and I didn't feel I owed any explanation to anyone. I was old enough to take care of myself! They could think whatever they wanted. I left.

The Long Way Home

Coincidentally, I learned of a transfer opportunity—just an hour up the road in the Raleigh office. One of my coworkers was accepting another position and encouraged me to apply. She told me that she knew I would get the job if I applied and invited me to move in with her and her two little girls—problem solved.

This could not have been timed any better! I applied for the job and was accepted as part of the import/export team for the company opening at their new offices. Everything in my world seemed to be back in place.

I moved to Raleigh, NC with this single mother of two girls and set up house. And though I was still working my day job, I became a sort of manny in exchange for room and board. Nothing illicit was happening between us. I needed a place to stay and a job, and she could give me those things. I offered her free babysitting. I was surviving.

A few days later, the phones started burning up when I did not show up in New York. Tommy finally got a hold of me as the heat was on and he was forced to give up the secret of my plan. That was okay with me because the job did not pan out the way I thought it would. My salary was strictly commission based again and thus, compensation lagged behind a few weeks. I was out of money.

Plus, I had started to not feel well physically. I thought it was maybe just the stress or what I had been eating, which was junk food. I would feel a stabbing pain on my side, starting late at night, but then it would go away.

I decided, much to my chagrin, that I would return home to upstate New York and regroup because I knew I certainly was not going to stay in North Carolina. I was happy to have found my freedom but being a teenager, broke and in pain was no way to live. I sold my car. Head down, tail between my legs, defeated—I returned home with the one-way ticket my dad bought me.

Burst My Bubble

My relationship with my mother was strained when I finally returned home. My father was fully entrenched in the church and the minister was meddling in our family affairs. And now I had to go back to that church and live by the house rules—like no smoking inside!

The minister had convinced me that my mother was the reason for the problems in the house. I was still angry with my mother for doing her Bible thumping to pull in Patricia, so I bought into the story when the minister started to tell me that my mother wasn't treating me right. All the while, the minister was being inappropriate with my father. Of course, my relationship with my mother was going to be strained!

My mother had been worrying about me all summer and now I was home, but in pain. Plus, there had been a storm a brewing up north with the minister and the church and my mom's friends from church. Mom and Dad were in marriage counseling.

My father was jovial and light-hearted without asking a lot of questions as they picked me up from the airport and brought me home. There were no bells and whistles for this homecoming. No welcome cake. My brother, living on his own at this point, did not even stop by to say hello. No surprise there.

Before my high school graduation and my Carolina Animal House mis-adventures, I had already accomplished all of the necessary paperwork to enter the Air Force on my next birthday, when I would turn seventeen in the fall. The Air Force was an easy decision for me. One: Blue was my favorite color back then and I liked the uniform better. Two: I hated camping, fishing, and outdoorsy roughing it, so the Army was a no-go. Three: The Navy was out because the thought of being out to sea for extended periods of time did not appeal to me, no matter how much I loved the ocean. Four: The Marines were not an option because, at the time, they resembled the kids who were bullying me in school—the loud, in-your-face macho type. The only long pole in the tent was that ONE parental signature that was required. I knew I had to tread lightly and be very persuasive to achieve this goal. I had to stay focused on my plan to get out—to be anywhere but here.

My dad kept pressing me, asking me what I was going to do now that I had graduated and was back in his house, without a job or money. Good question, Dad! After he began to lose patience with my lack of vision, I finally laid my intentions on him. I suggested joining the military. Without skipping a beat, he thought it was an admirable idea! Well, hooray. That was easier than I anticipated. No doubt Dad was relieved, as he and Mom had certainly not made any plans to pay for college or any job training or money toward purchasing a home, or anything to help my future survival. That didn't happen for my older brother. No reason it was happening for me. We were literally thrown into the deep end of the pool of life. Good luck! Sink or swim. Oh, don't worry—I would swim, and swim I did.

However, my dad did know it was going to be a challenge to get it approved by my mother. My mother was going through some stuff with her older son drinking and shacking up with a girl (not cool with any Fundamentalist church opinion of parenting skills), Dad was having some kind of special relationship with the church minister that was getting all up in Mom's business, and I was still only on the edge of seventeen years old and had disappeared for the whole summer. One step at a time. I had my father in my corner. This was a great feeling!

Mom wanted to be something she wasn't. She wanted to be respected by the church, the neighbors, her family. She tried so hard to live up to standards that were always just out of reach. Our house was in the eye of the hurricane and disturbing forces were swirling around and were bound to hit sometime. I knew Mom wouldn't want her baby boy in the military, but she had everything to lose if Dad and the church agreed that this was the best option for me.

I needed beer in order to endure the purgatory of home—and that required money. Suddenly, there I was, back at my old job at McDonald's. The entire crew was still there, and I picked up where I left off. It felt like I never left, actually. But something was off. I had begun to lose my appetite and was rapidly losing weight.

I left work early one day, gripping my side, as I told the shift manager I did not feel well. I had been vomiting in the men's room. I thought maybe it was just the flu or something, but I could not explain the sharp piercing pain in my right side above my hip and lower stomach.

That night I was invited to one of my work friend's new apartment a few miles down the road, where I knew there would be plenty of free beer and alcohol. My mom was out for the evening and my dad was watching TV as I breezed through the living room on my way out to the party.

In under an hour, I returned home and my dad was just as surprised as I was. He wanted to know what was wrong with the party. I told him I was not feeling well, as I held my side and told him I was heading to bed. He encouraged bed, stating it must just be gas. My mother came home and, apparently, my dad informed her of the uncharacteristic behavior of their youngest son missing the opportunity to go to a party.

Mom came in and woke me up asking me what was wrong. I told her and pointed to where the pain was coming from. My mother had completed a few years of nursing school and knew just enough, probably as a mother, about what the problem could be. However, she would never get treatment through the family budget approval process, as my dad's policy was that we did not go to doctors, dentists, or lawyers. He didn't on the farm and he didn't see the need for it now that he was living in a city house.

"Sleep it off, drink more water, it's just gas," my father diagnosed. My mom would try to heal everything with pink Pepto-Bismol, but this time the chalky pink stuff was not working its magic. "I don't think it's gas, Mark.

I think it's your appendix." I did fall back asleep, but woke up in the middle of the night, vomiting green bile. I knew something was wrong.

In that moment I took full charge of the situation, throwing open my parents' bedroom door and announcing sharply and loudly that I was going to the hospital! Either they could take me or I was taking a taxi! Something was wrong! Mom jumped out of bed and got dressed. I don't think Dad even said a word.

When I arrived at the hospital and finally got to see a doctor, the panic in his eyes led to a diagnosis of a nearly exploded appendix! The doctor knew that I must've been in a tremendous amount of pain. He was a nice man, "You're going to be alright, son, hang in there. I promise you in a few hours this will all go away." And as I leaned over the bed, I barfed green bile on his shoes, like something out of *The Exorcist*.

Within a matter of minutes, I was taken into emergency surgery to have my appendix removed. I had never been to the hospital or even had a broken bone. It was weird to me that after the surgery, the pain left immediately. Odd, I thought to myself, they took out the organ that was causing the pain, but the suture, the incision area, hurt like hell. Because I was underage (fake IDs don't work in a hospital), they were reluctant to give me painkillers. No painkillers? You have got to be kidding me! That really pissed me off.

My own version of Nurse Ratched went to my mother and warned her that she thought I was addicted to drugs. I was seeking painkillers ALL the time, she told my mother. I could hear my mother and this nurse having this conversation and I was thinking, "Hello, you crazy people, I just had surgery! *That's* why I'm in pain. *NO*... I do not want to binge on pain medicine! I had my appendix out five minutes ago, you stupid nurse!" But I didn't say any of that aloud. I thought Mom would defend me and get me the good stuff. Nope! My mom agreed. The nurse said, "Let's give him a baby aspirin; he'll be fine." Unbelievable! They would later compare Bible study notes in my room, while I am sure I rolled my eyes reeling in pain and utter disbelief.

After the hospital, I went home to recover on the sofa in the living room. The sofa was easier to reach than my upstairs all red, Coca-Cola-themed bed-room. Plus, I could see and hear everything going on in the house. I was fussed over for a bit, but that quickly wore off. Meanwhile, I was frantically trying to get a hold of my Air Force recruiter, as my seventeenth birthday was near. My plan was to get out of Dodge and start my life!!

When I finally got in touch with him, he delivered the bad news: I would not be able to join the Air Force or leave for boot camp until I received a release from my surgeon. I was devastated. I pleaded with him and told him I was just fine and I was ready to go. I would sign any papers he needed at this point. He told me the decision was no longer his; it was up to the medical board.

I was stuck. I hated being back home. But after a few weeks, I got my strength back and returned to work. My manager at McDonald's felt horrible. The day I asked to go home, she thought I was just hungover from drinking too much with her and the other managers. She did not realize how seriously I was in pain. We laughed about it, and I got back to work on a full-time schedule. I decided I was going to put my head down and just work as much as I could to distract me from the time it was going to take for me to get cleared to join the Air Force.

A Family Deconstructed

While I was still in the hospital, I learned that Mom had decided her marriage was over. My dad had been unusually distant—stopping by only once to visit me in the hospital. I knew he was spending a lot of time away from the house, but a divorce?

This was a devastating blow to our family. My parents worried, "What would the neighbors think? What would the people at church say?"

September (my six-month waiting period to be cleared by the medical board) could not come fast enough. "I've got to get out of here! Anywhere but here!" was beating like a silent drum in my soul.

I just didn't understand the idea of my parents divorcing. Mom was too sad to talk, taking one day at a time. When I asked my dad why as I sat recovering on the couch in the living room, he paused for a minute. Not even turning around to look at me, he said with exhaustion "Why what, Mark? What do you want me to tell you?" He turned his head and we both just starred at each other, silent. He continued walking upstairs and that was the last time we would ever speak about the divorce.

My brother had already moved out of the house. My mom grabbed this opportunity to rent out the spare room to a young couple with children who were in need. That was how Mom coped best. If she could help another couple with a perceived greater need, she could shelve her own feelings. The quiet house was now suddenly filled with activity again, hustle and bustle, with two young girls full of energy. Perfect—any distraction would be better than to address the dead stinking carcass in the living room called conflict. In our house, we just moved it around, and sprinkled the carpet with deodorizer to cover up the smell.

I think an important life lesson was badly missed at this juncture in my life. I felt guilty because I was the "less than" member of the family and somehow felt the divorce was partly my fault. Everyone was ganging up on my mother and yet ultimately, they left her. She had prayed for years to have her whole family "saved" by coming to church with her. Now that everyone was in church, she lost all control. Her husband was carrying on with the minister. Her older son moved out and was living in sin. Her younger son was going into the military. I felt guilty because I had told the minister information about my home life which led to the minister concluding that my mother was a poor parent. I felt like I needed to do something to show her she was loved.

I moved heaven and earth working at McDonald's and other odd jobs to get my mother a new car that she could afford—to help her get on with her new life. She never had a new car. If I could get her that car, then I could leave for boot camp and everything would be okay.

So there I was, a punk-ass kid of seventeen, walking into a Pontiac dealership, plunking down every penny I had saved on a deposit, plates, and car insurance for a new Sunbird. And I made arrangements for low monthly payments that my mother could afford.

I should have been saving my earnings for my own future and the expenses I would have going into the military. But I didn't.

I realize now that as a form of support because I felt sorry for her, I just fed her victimization role. Years later, when Mom had spent all the money from the sale of the house (that she got in the divorce) on living a decadent life, I would realize enabling her was the exact opposite of what I should have been doing. I loved her, yes, but I should not have encouraged the excuses and deflection of responsibility of her role in the failed marriage and shattered family.

Right before I left for the Air Force, Mom had a new young family renting a room in our house. I was sure this new family would be there to love Mom. Their little girls were adorable and just as pure as new life itself. The girls used to call me "Magic Mark-er," because I sat on the floor and colored with them for hours when I was home.

My childhood home became nothing more than a pit stop; somewhere to shower and change when I was in town. The rooms were all rented and occupied. My brother and I left the shredded, chilly nest; the nest that was no longer fit for a family. My father became cold and indifferent, my mother depressed and self-absorbed. My parents barely paid any attention to their two grown boys. Within a few years the house was sold and my mother moved to Albany.

It was a painful time. I hurt.

In the midst of all of this, my father and the minister went on a trip to Cape Cod. There, the minister died in his arms of kidney failure. It made me wonder about God and consequences for the minister's behavior in the preceding years.

As the ink dried on my parent's divorce papers and the flowers began to wilt on the minister's grave, Dad would not be alone for long. He soon remarried a woman from the church. Oddly enough, I remember my mother had counseled her on being a better wife and mother. Dad's soon-to-be wife had recently finalized her own divorce before she married my father. She had two young children from her first marriage and would later give birth to a new brother.

To Mom with Love

I felt partially responsible for my parents' divorce. I reinforced the minister's mission to prove my mom was not a good parent. After my dad left, I was home trying to help Mom keep it all together while never really talking about the dead moose in the living room called her divorce. Instead I helped skirt around it, and through my own guilt, tried to help her put the pieces back together. By this time, she was forced to find a job, as the divorce not only caused a strain on our family dynamics but also caused a strain on the financial situation. She began working in a doctor's office in the next city over, near the hospital where I had my appendix taken out.

Right before I left for boot camp, I snuck the keys off her key ring to get into my mother's new office in Saratoga Springs, New York. On her desk I left her a homemade inspirational tape of music I had recorded just for her. She and my father had just split up and were heading straight for a divorce. I knew she was going through a tough time and it was going to be even more difficult for her, letting her seventeen-year-old son go off to boot camp.

I was (and still am) fond of creating homemade mix tapes/music (now called playlists) that speak to situations in life at that moment. It was music to inspire and reassure my friends and family, and I would spend hours mixing and matching songs.

At this time, the hit song by Patti LaBelle and Michael McDonald that was topping the charts was "On My Own." I thought this was fitting as our family of four was splitting up and going in separate directions to start our own individual lives. But it was not as romantic as it sounds.

On my mom's cassette tape, the first song was "There's a Winner in You" by Patti LaBelle. The words of the song were uplifting for someone going through so much heartache. The song is about someone who is down in the dumps and needs a friend to talk them through this hard patch in their life. It also encouraged one to pull themselves up by the bootstraps and move forward from whatever life has dealt them. It's the kind of song a friend would give, versus one coming from her youngest son. Looking back now, it was a nice gesture, something that would be remembered by my mother. However, the life lesson was not necessarily fully learned by either of us. I left the tape with flowers on her desk. I had already offered her some other advice prior to my departure. In the end, while she did recognize the gift and flowers, I did not feel that she understood the full impact of the lesson being taught in the lyrics.

After dropping off my gift, I went back home, tidied up my boxes of childhood memories, and finished packing. A few of my girl friends from McDonald's were having a small send-off party for me that night. I got home at a reasonable hour to try to get some sleep before leaving for Albany early the next morning. Mom would take me.

Wild Blue Yonder

I was seventeen years old and beginning a totally new phase of my life. The sun was still summer warm and the breeze had a fall sharp crispness. Everything felt so clean. A fresh start. I was about to head to boot camp for six weeks.

I'd been planning this day for a very long time. I was anxious to just be there already, but nervous about what I would find once I arrived. It was bittersweet to be leaving on a new adventure that I knew would change my life, when my childhood home was literally falling apart. I felt guilty and relieved. It was odd, at best, to have your emotions thrown in a blender, with no one to talk about them with.

Dad stopped by before I left to say goodbye and it was tense. Not tense that I was leaving, but tense because we didn't know how to talk to each other. I waited for my brother to come by or call me. Secretly, I was hoping he would be at the small send-off party. He never showed, which should not have been a surprise since he had been an absentee brother up to this point. What I had hoped for was romanticized anyway and it was probably best that he didn't come because it would have led to more disappointment.

That morning, as I prepared to leave, I looked at myself in the mirror, squared my shoulders, imagined great things for myself, and walked my luggage out to the car, determined not to let my brother's disconnection or the entire dysfunctionality of the past couple of years get me down. I was large and in charge of my destiny now. "Can we get there already?" I impatiently said to myself. Not to boot camp, but to the greatness of my destiny.

Mom came out, we got in the car, and off we went, headed to Albany from my small hometown of the Village of Ballston Spa. The journey was filled with small talk and chit chat, "Did you pack this? Did you remember that?" Again, we did not talk about real life.

My mother dropped me off in downtown Albany, wiping tears from her eyes and hugging me, as she left me at the Military Entrance Processing Station (MEPS) where I would officially enter the military. I was a little embarrassed but it was okay, and kind of cool actually to have someone there. Some of the kids did not have anyone with them.

"I love you, Mark," she whispered as I faded away into the sea of recruits.

From there our group of young recruits, chattering away with nervous energy, boarded a bus to New Jersey, then a plane to San Antonio, Texas, only to board another bus to take us to Lackland Air Force Base, on the outskirts of San Antonio. We would be greeted by a "welcoming committee" of drill instructors. I had no clue what that would be like, but knew it was about to get real. The nerves were so intense, I could have puked.

Aim High

We hurried and scurried; a quiet and thoughtful group disembarked at Lackland Air Force Base, the gateway to the Air Force for all those who enlisted, and the only Air Force boot camp. We were tired—by design, I think. It was late at night by the time we rolled up to Basic Military Training.

We lined up on the blue line adjacent to the bus and plopped our luggage down. I could see in some of the drill sergeants' eyes that our arrival was not going well. Then this "welcoming committee" of drill sergeants went crazy ballistic, screaming, and hollering. I could barely make out what they were saying. It quickly became evident that we were being instructed to get back on the bus and do it again. Do what again? I wondered in my sleepy mind. I followed along, but it was scary.

After about the fourth time, someone whispered the secret that spread like wildfire, a clue to what they were waiting for. We were expected to get off the bus quickly and hold our bags. Then we'd wait for the obvious signal from the first person to the last to gently place the bags down on the blue line in one motion and one whispering gentle sound. It worked. I often wondered how long they would have let us stay out there that night.

We were instructed to get upstairs and find a bunk, place our luggage in the closet on the wall next to the bunk, and get to bed "quickly." It was very quiet and everyone moved with purpose and speed. I quickly brushed my teeth and jumped into bed, which was a hard mattress, a sheet, and wool blanket with a lumpy, stinky pillow. I didn't care, I was exhausted from the surge of adrenaline and emotionally drained.

It felt like the six weeks of boot camp were going to be insurmountable. I was from rural, upstate New York and boot camp was a microcosm of all different walks of life and society—expected to unite and walk the same path in uniform. There were about sixty guys in a boot camp team, which the Air Force called a "flight."

I quickly discovered that boot camp is designed to break us down—to bring us down to ground zero and then build us back up as a cohesive team with survival skills, as members of the military. These are skills, if learned correctly, that we'd take with us for the rest of our lives. The lessons guided us to be self-starters, to encourage each other, to increase our own self-discipline, to act with integrity, and to provide excellence in all we do: "service before self." I embraced the structure. The clearly defined parameters and rules were something I could wrap my head around and embrace. Unlike my childhood home, the environment was not passive aggressive nor an emotional minefield.

I don't think I was a particularly stellar airman, but I had a desire to excel and the motivation to succeed. Overall, boot camp was a true leadership and learning experience that would shape my life path going forward.

In addition to the physical fitness, teamwork was a big challenge. I learned I liked marching. I had never been exposed to this particular skill, so I think I shocked myself! I was really good at instructing drill and marching—to the point where I led our flight to marching challenge championships. It was rewarding to be supported by the team and it was comforting to not be picked on. Even when I did make a mistake, the rest of the team championed my efforts so we would go on to reach victory in the competition. This true sense of brotherhood and bonding made me feel complete.

House Mouse

There were additional assigned duties while you were in boot camp, such as dorm guard, latrine guard, and kitchen duty. And then there was one job in particular that nobody wanted, the House Mouse, the drill sergeant's assistant who was tasked with being the sergeant's eyes and ears—quiet, and never seen. And, of course, as much as I diverted any eye contact with the drill sergeant, I heard, "Gibson, you're the House Mouse." *Son of a....* Even my fellow teammates patted me on the shoulder after he was not looking as a sign of condolence and solidarity.

The House Mouse had to report in to the drill instructor, in addition to all the normal morning tasks. My duties included posting the flight's administrative duties for the day, calculating demerits, and keeping account of all the administrative details.

As the assistant to the drill instructor, I spent a lot of time with him. Well, most people didn't want *that* much attention from the drill instructor or to have to adhere to an additional set of rules when interacting with a higher-ranked individual—rules such as keeping one's uniform impeccable, not speaking unless spoken to, following etiquette, or using proper speaking tone, order, and language. It was a nerve-racking assignment for most people and I was the chosen one. Great!

But I kind of liked it. It was cool to me. I learned a lot—even though I don't think I ever looked him directly in the eyes. I liked it because I was "special." In many of my fellow airmen's minds, I was the closest individual to this untamed beast. They would ask me questions, wanting to know what he was like and what we talked about. I felt like a big shot.

As House Mouse, my cot was right outside the drill instructor's door. No one was allowed out of bed until reveille sounded each morning. Everyone had to have an equal amount of time to do morning tasks (brush teeth, shower, make bed, and get dressed), so no one would have an unfair advantage over anyone else. If, like me, you had extra morning duties, you still had to figure out how to get it all done within the specified amount of time.

The punishment for not finishing on time was that the entire flight had to go back and do it all over again, so everyone would learn to finish at the same time. If you were in a combat situation and couldn't get packed up to go on time, your delay could literally kill people. The peer pressure was intense. This practice encouraged teamwork; if you saw someone struggling, others could jump in so the goal of group finishing on time would be achieved. Cooperate and graduate! Break us down as individuals; build us up as a team.

A unique and unexpected benefit of boot camp was finding a deeper appreciation of Patti LaBelle's music. Her lyrics became the soundscape of boot camp. When the drill instructor arrived at 5 a.m. to do paperwork, he played Patti LaBelle and that's what the entire flight woke up to. No one was permitted to get out of bed until reveille, but they could still hear LaBelle playing from the office. I would try to predict which tape he would play, since it was part of my job to keep them all organized and stacked alphabetically.

Years later, when I realized how Patti would come in and out of my life, intentionally or unintentionally, I found that she was actually very influential, seemingly speaking to my personal experiences with her words. In fact, one day later in life for my birthday, my partner, whom I affectionately call "Mr. Wonderful," arranged for me to actually meet Patti LaBelle and dance and sing with her on stage.

Tech School

After graduating from boot camp, I was shipped out to Keesler Air Force Base in Biloxi, Mississippi, to go through several weeks of technical school. My classes were in computer, administration, and typing. You had to be proficient in these technical skills before you'd receive your first assignment. It wasn't hard, there was just a precise formula and course work that had to be accomplished. I was up for the challenge.

At Christmas, we were ordered home on mandatory blanket leave, where everyone was forced to take leave at the same time since the school shut down. It was odd to return to my childhood home. I guess it never occurred to me that I could go on leave anywhere in the world, but the magnetic pull took me back to upstate New York.

When I arrived, the place felt broken and tattered. I finally saw the house through an outsider's eyes. I wondered what Tommy and my other friends thought of my home when we were younger. To further make it feel less like home, my stuff had been either moved or sold to make more room for renters. What hurt the most was that my mom had sold my fish tanks and all of the supplies that I had packed and stored away. In my mind, I had planned to send for them later when I had my own new place. My mother had let a drug dealer who was dating one of her friends move in to stay occasionally, and he must have gone off with my stuff, she explained.

The total disregard for my property felt like a penance I had to pay because I left.

Upon seeing what remained of my home, I left, hurt and despondent. Certainly, there were beers to be had with the old posse to drown my sorrows. I remember I went looking for my brother as well, but he dodged me like the emotional bullet I was. He didn't want to confront the obvious disintegration of our family or be obligated to recognize I was doing something positive with my life.

My trips home would become less frequent after this, but guilt always managed to bring me home for Christmas. Mom was alone and her momma's boy was not going to let his mother spend Christmas without family. Throughout my entire military career, I always made sure we were together for Christmas unless I was deployed.

Where is Why-Oming?

When you finish tech school, you receive your first permanent assignment. This is a big event. When I hurriedly opened my envelope to look at my assignment, it said I was going to F.E. Warren Air Force Base, NY. I knew loosely about New York bases, but I didn't know this one. I knew there was one in the north near Canada, one on the west side of the state, but where was this F.E. Warren? Inquisitively, I approached the woman at the counter and asked her to show me on the map where this base was. She told me that my sheet had a typo. My assignment was not in *N-Y*. It was in *W-Y*.

I was going to Wyoming! I didn't know where the hell Wyoming was! Looking at me with a scornful "you small-town hick" look, she took her really long yardstick and smacked it on the map, to the center of the country to show me Cheyenne, Wyoming. Oh crap!

I joined the military to get out of town and see the world, but I admit I was pretty apprehensive and nervous to go that far across the country, away from my family, to live in what seemed to be the middle of nowhere. "Why Wyoming, though?" I thought.

In elementary school, five years old

With grandparents (ten years old)

BALLSTON JOURNAL   JUNE 24, 1981   Page 5

Students helping students in Burnt Hills-Ballston Lake

Recently, BH-BL students who are involved in the PEER Assistance Program joined with program coordinators, Edward Warren, David Guilmette and Barbara Oberdieck in a weekend of intensive training which included enhancing communicative skills and personal and interpersonal relationship activities.

Elliot Masie, of the National Humanistic Education Center, Sagamore Institute, conducted the workshop at Skye Farm, Warrensburg. Masie is an experienced consultant in leadership development, student activities, and creative problem solving.

The Peer Assistance Program began in the Burnt Hills-Ballston Lake School System in the Spring of 1980 and now operates at all levels within the district. "Students helping students" is the basic principle upon which the program is based. This principle is implemented by students being trained to assist other students in the development of a value system, ventilaiton of feelings, building a decision-making process, learning to accept responsibility, and developing better interpersonal relationships.

This school year, the "peers" have been involved in a variety of projects including offering a very well received exercise on building self-esteem in many of the elementary classrooms, assisting in the tenth grade orientation program in the high school, presentarions in junior high Home Economics and Health classes, and acting as facilitators for the sixth grade substance abuse program. A new phase of the program is labeled "one-to-ones," wherein "peers" are assigned to be a "buddy" to a fellow student, offering him/her an opportunity to ventilate, "cool off," and/or sort things out.

One of the program's coordinators, Edward Warren, who is also the principal of the BH-BL Senior High School, has stated that the program is "a

tremendous undertaking; but we are hoping that the Peer Assistance Program will be the impetus, and a new sense of caring and sharing will snowball throughout the district." The other two coordinators of the program, high school Sociology teacher, David Guilmette, and Barbara Oberdieck, a couselor who comes into the district from Catholic Family Services of Saratoga through funding from Community Human Services, agree that the program is developing "a climate of caring and mutual concern within the school."

The costs of operating the program have been met by fund raising activities of the "peers" themselves, a generous donation from the six principals of the BH-BL school district, and the BH-HL Community Human Services. The CHS contribution was made possible through funds raised by the Mayfair Women's Club at their Spring Fashion Show and Card Party.

Exchange vows

Mr and Mrs Kenneth Brooner of Mesa, Arizona announce the marriage of their daughter, Karen Lynn, to Paul Tracy Danison. Mr Danison is the son of Mr and Mrs Robert C Danison of Ballston Spa.

The marriage took place on May 24 in Los Gatos, California at the home of Mr and Mrs Richard Hall, sister of the bride.

Mrs Danison is a graduate of Evansville University, Indiana. Mr Danison is a graduate of the University of Buffalo and is continuing graduate studies at the University of Chicago.

MARK GIBSON of Ballston Avenue was the top collector in a recent Skate-a-thon for the Muscular Dystrophy Association. The twelve-year-old skated 3 hours and collected $342.48. The event took place at the Star Burst in Clifton Park and 100 skaters participated.

Roller-skating championship MDA trophy from 1981

BALLSTON SPA MIDDLE SCHOOL
MARK GIBSON
STUDENT
RD #5 Ballston Sp
ADDRESS
11/21/68
DATE OF BIRTH   GRADE
Blue
COLOR EYES HAIR   BLOOD TYPE

My middle school ID card from 1980

The Wonder Years

Wild, Wild West

Life was easier then, I packed up my suitcase and military-issued duffel bag and headed out. My one small box of personal items, books, and cassettes, etc., was mailed ahead of time to my sponsor at F.E. Warren. A sponsor is someone assigned to you who helps answer questions while you transition and assists you when you arrive at a new duty station. Typically, when one joins the military they have not accumulated a vast amount of household goods. Besides, most of what I did have was no longer in storage in my closet back home in upstate New York.

I left the small Albany airport, literally walked out onto the flight-line to climb stairs to board the plane. Earlier in my teens I picked up the smoking habit so I was seated in the back of the plane with the smokers. At this point, this was the longest flight of my life, with many connections, but I was excited to turn this page and really start anew.

I was promoted to Airman First Class after boot camp which was two stripes on my sleeve. This was an automatic promotion for those enlisted who upgraded their initial enlistment from four to six years. After successful completion of technical school, my initial title was Administrative Specialist; my title would change after successful completion of continued education and time in a functional job. I was assigned to a Munitions Maintenance Squadron and my office was in a nuclear weapons storage area. Talk about an eye-opening experience! This was the area on the backside of the base, where they housed the peacekeeper nuclear missiles when they came in for maintenance. The peacekeeper had ten nuclear warheads in the nose and was mammoth in size.

Ironically, I wanted to see the world yet here I was sitting in an office, right next to the missiles that could destroy the entire planet with the push of a button. But no pressure.

To reach my office each day I ran a gauntlet of *Get Smart*-style doors, hand scans, eye scans, code words, and keys. Code words changed daily. I was in a top secret facility, doing "If I told you what I'm doing, I'd have to kill you" work with deep cover officials. I would've written home to Mom about my adventures, but then they could accuse me of treason.

My supervisor in the squadron, a sergeant, was a gruff, slightly older guy. At Keesler, they taught us that your sergeant was usually pretty much God, and you were to fear and obey him (it was usually a him back then). This was not that situation. His name was Sergeant Williams. He had curly red hair, a face full of freckles and hailed from Cleveland, Ohio. He smoked Marlboro cigarettes and drank Jim Beam like it was water. He was our boss. He didn't live in the dorm. Instead, he lived in a very small trailer, with a cat, in a trailer court off base on the South Greeley Highway. A typical bachelor pad with cigarette butts and pizza crusts all around, it stunk to high heaven. Contrary to most images of military personnel, he was not as rigid as you'd expect.

My first active duty assignment also brought my first male encounter with a fellow airman on base. We had a shared secret interest (sex) and we were interested in each other! This was not casual for me. I really cared for this man. We became very close, but it was hard to find time to be together. Between all the cameras and security at the base and spending time living in the same community, there was a lot of pent-up frustration along with the sexual tension and excitement of planning and waiting for opportunities.

Love Connections

I began hanging out at Sergeant Williams's house after work and on weekends to drink beer and watch TV. I was still underage but most people didn't question it or care back then, the attitude was if you can serve your country you can have a beer.

On one visit, I heard Sarge talking to his girlfriend, Suzy, back in Cleveland, Ohio. I actually couldn't believe that he would make that drive from Wyoming to Ohio to see his girlfriend. Often. He must have really loved her.

Sergeant Williams and his girlfriend had been dating for a very long time. I think they were even high school sweethearts. Suzy would come out to Wyoming a few times to visit. Soon Suzy started telling me about her roommate back in Cleveland. Her name was Lisa. I was told that she was going to come out for a visit, and Williams and Suzy convinced me to have Lisa stay at my place. By that time, I had bought a trailer off base and lived across the trailer park from Sarge. My trailer was bigger and cleaner. No cigarette butts or pizza crusts at my place, and it certainly didn't smell like a locker room.

The Albany Bar was just over the bridge that brought you into Cheyenne, and Williams was going to pick up Lisa and Suzy down in Denver. He had a small sports car and there wouldn't be enough room for me to go, especially with all their luggage, he told me. He was going to bring the girls back and we would meet at the bar. I think it was a forced opportunity to meet a girl of substance who was pretty, and so full of life and energy. She had a laugh that was truly special.

Marry the Gay Away

Lisa visited around the Thanksgiving holiday, the weekend of my nineteenth birthday. To celebrate my birthday, we drank kamikaze shots (a LOT of them) at the Albany Bar. Since Albany, New York, was in the general vicinity of where I grew up, it seemed appropriate to be at the Albany Bar in Wyoming for my birthday if I couldn't be home. Lisa and I nursed a hangover the rest of the weekend—watching movies, making food, and getting to know each other.

Lisa and I made a really good couple, full of positive energy. We were fun together. Lisa took quickly to the military lifestyle. We had lots of friends. She took on the loyalty and friendship badge for sad and lonely airmen. She would never let any one of them sit in the dorm alone for a holiday or birthday. Instead, we would host parties and dinners for the guys when she visited.

Lisa and I dated long distance, which people said wouldn't last, but I was determined! We commuted, talked on the phone, and wrote love letters. I would drive the nearly twenty-hour trip from Cheyenne to Cleveland to see her. I would surprise her. I would go spend long weekends with her. It's actually amazing that there were no car crashes, because I did crazy unsafe things to get there in record time. We made it work.

After about a year of long-distance dating, Lisa and I decided to move in together. She moved to Cheyenne from Cleveland, found a job, and settled in. Within a year, I finally asked her to marry me, but I knew what was going on deep down inside. I was gay, and I was trying to talk myself into not being gay because I was in the military. If I got married then I couldn't be gay. I was sealing the deal. If I got married this would force me to stop the affair with the man at the base. But this was going to be difficult because I was falling hard for him. We were together a lot. I guess I thought that because I would be happy being married to Lisa, it wouldn't hurt so much that I wasn't getting the relationship I dreamed of.

The constant turmoil in my mind about trying not to be gay was temporarily abated by thinking that if I was with a woman and I was married AND I was in the military, it just wasn't possible that I was gay. That's all there was to it.

I regret that I dragged another person into my turmoil. My only true regret in life.

I Do (and Don't)

We had a big, fancy wedding with over one hundred guests in Cleveland, Ohio. It was a grand event. My family and friends came from New York. I felt odd knowing that I wasn't really being true to myself at this point. I wanted to do anything to be "normal" and to stop this downward guilt spiral. I was doing what was expected of me but what I really felt deep down was sadness, fear, guilt, and that I was a fraud. Inauthentic.

My brother was the best man by default. He wasn't MY best man. It was only for appearances; for my wife's side of the family. Her mother insisted that of course it was traditional that the groom would have his brother or father as best man. And, of course, you would invite friends to be groomsmen versus having a best friend as a best man. I was in such a downward spiral that the assumption was to just follow and get out of the way, the end result would land me a marriage and I could break these chains that were causing so much hurt inside.

The bachelor party was fun. My brother did all right in that regard. We went to a Major League baseball game in a bus limo. I hated baseball, but everyone else thought it would be fun. Straight guys like professional sports and I was getting married so I would like professional sports. That's the way it works, right? Later that night, we drove around in this huge limo with beers flowing, and we hit strip clubs and porn adult bookstores. So cliché.

I was drunk and tired and could not wait to get back to the hotel. With so many childhood and military friends that I was emotionally, physically, or sexually involved with at some point, I felt like a long-tailed cat in a room full of rocking chairs. The audacity, I thought to myself, but then again, the justification was to silently prove to them that I was getting married and the past was in the past.

I bid everyone good night and left them in the bar in the lobby, and not long after taking a shower, there was a knock at the door. I answered in a towel still wet. The visitor used a sportsman-like maneuver to tackle me in a friendly way (like we used to when we were "curious" teenagers) and threw me on the bed. I thought this was so awkward and strange as I was about to get married the following day. But I could not resist.

He snuck out of my room and moments later there was another knock on the door. This time, in just underwear, I answered. I thought it was my tackle man coming back. Shocked and utterly surprised, it was the true love that I was leaving behind. He wanted to talk and I agreed. He spent the night as we passed out in a heap in each other's arms. I remember waking up in a panic as my brother was pounding on the door. I thought I had overslept. How was I going to explain or get rid of him?

I jumped into shorts and a T-shirt and barreled out the door. I rushed past my brother so he would follow and made my way to the elevator saying that I needed a cigarette and a Diet Coke—badly.

I was so caught off guard with my evening visitors that I rushed into the day. I still had to get ready for my wedding. I jumped into my white tux, but hungover from bachelor party debauchery and my late-night visitors, I forgot to shave. Everyone else made their way to the church. My brother and I went in a separate limo ordered just for the groom. I can't even remember what we talked about, if we talked at all. I was so nervous, I was chain-smoking cigarettes. The limo pulled up in back of the church and I remember burning my white tux coat tails with the cigarette as I got out of the car. I was a wreck.

My brother summoned Mom, who quickly went into MacGyver mode. She ransacked a desk in the church's office in the back and found liquid Wite-Out. I remember she was painting on my tux as the priest was talking to me about the ceremony. I am sure it looked like a skit out of *The Beverly Hillbillies*.

As trusting as Lisa was, she was not difficult to fool. I think she always suspected that I was gay. I'd had encounters with women as an adolescent to assure me that so long as I was free to fantasize I could provide the illusion of heterosexuality and "rise to any occasion." But the toll of this deception and the challenge to keep up the charade eventually built to an explosive level.

When Lisa and I returned from our fabulous two-week honeymoon in Hawaii, we settled into a nice life as the perfect hosts—the role model military husband and wife. It wasn't long before my plan of denying my sexuality was torn to shreds.

Top Secret

The relationship that developed with my military man back at F.E. Warren was not just a sexual dalliance. I fell in love with this man, and there I was, married to a woman. He was married and had a kid on the way. We worked on base and were inseparable. We were all so young.

Like Lisa, he was a Midwesterner and had a very laid-back approach to life; he was not easily shaken. He treated me very well and never, or should I say only in my wildest dreams, would I imagine we would have a secretive affair. This was *Brokeback Mountain* before the movie.

He told me one night, while I was lying in his arms, looking into my eyes, "I love you, Mark. I really love you." I felt sick. I couldn't sleep. I didn't know what to do with this information. I was married after all. Hell, so was he.

In the military, there are many secrets. Security clearance is required for action, for knowledge, for advancement. You learn how to compartmentalize. For me, keeping my private life private was the *real* top secret security work.

I genuinely liked this man and was afraid to admit, I was falling in love with him, and couldn't help but envision a life with him, free of the constraints of the shame and secrecy. When I discovered a longtime family friend was also sleeping with this guy, I was devastated. I don't think I thought there was enough alcohol in the world to stop this amount of pain, betrayal, and hurt. They had met at MY wedding! How could my life possibly get any more bizarre?

No stranger to guilt and shame, I internalized this imagined betrayal as my just desserts, given the life of deception I was living with my wife. Not only was he cheating on his wife with me, but now he was essentially cheating on me with my family friend. Numbing the hurt and confusion about my life choices, I began drinking more and more. Drinking wasn't interfering with my life at that point, but the secrecy was. I would drink to forget.

Operation Escape

Things started heating up in the Middle East and before we knew it, Saddam Hussein became a household name. I was actually excited to learn about pending deployment opportunities and began to volunteer for everything, as I was itching to get off base. Four years in any one spot is a long time with regard to military standards, and I desperately needed a change in scenery to assess my emotional landscape.

Sure enough, I was picked for a deployment to Operation Desert Shield, which would prove to be the spin up to Desert Storm. I deployed to Riyadh, Saudi Arabia, for a few months and loved the freedom to leave the looming temptations of my secrets behind in Cheyenne. I was lonely and sad, but for different reasons than that of my fellow airmen. They were truly lonely for their wives and kids. Sure, I would call home for regular morale calls and talk with my wife, friends, and family, but I loved the freedom the deployment offered by way of relieving steam in the pressure cooker of my mind. "Gibson, only you would go the desert to relieve steam and pressure," I thought to myself. But hey, it was working.

I was thousands of miles away from home but kept thinking about being married and my desire for men. And as long as I was deployed, I didn't have to deal with the day-to-day issues of being married, having sex, or thinking about children.

Music played a great part in keeping me company while deployed. I was listening to a Garth Brooks song ("The River") when I had a sudden longing to speak to my father. I reached out and we had a particularly poignant talk. I was seeking his approval to launch the next bright idea I had brewing in my mind: to invest in real estate. He had no experience in the field but thought it was obtainable, and he cautioned me that the stakes were higher the larger the investments. This was insightful to a twenty-year-old young man, as I took most things on face value and I was reading a how-to book on purchasing investment properties with no to low money down.

To distract myself from the overwhelming sadness, I filled my free time with this new interest. Because of the heat, I worked at night when it was cooler. I only needed about three or four hours of sleep, so during the day, I took a video and cassette real estate course on flipping houses. I told Lisa that when I came home, we'd start investing in real estate. I don't think Lisa believed me. I don't think she was worried about money the way I was.

Being deployed is tough on the mind, because every day seems like the same as the next or last—same routines, job, auto function, and daily exercise. Even the food is the same. Riyadh was hot and miserable with chances of hot and miserable forecast upon you.

I excelled in my job. I worked at the postal unit with a group of people who were actually fun. We got to bust the boxes of contraband being shipped into the country, so we kept the booze and porn; right after we told the officials we would dispose of the contraband properly. In the theater of war, there are military laws you had to adhere to, including no drinking.

The time flew by and it was not long until my four months was over and I was on my way home to Cheyenne. I was just learning, or should I say growing accustomed, to developing quick friends/relationships and having to bid them farewell as a common way of life in the military. That did not make it any easier; it just became a way of life. Everything in the military routine was systematic; I learned it well, adapted, and adjusted quickly.

I remember coming home procedures. Reentry instructions for the family were given in great detail. This was pre-PTSD (Post-Traumatic Stress Disorder) and paved the way for allowing the service member to reenter home life slowly. Instructions even included how to handle sex. The counselors warned the military members and the spouses that sex may not be the same or it may take a while to get back into the groove of things. (So to speak.) Phew, I was off the hook for a little while. We had been married for a few years and I was convinced Lisa was trying to trap me into having a child, by encouraging me to forget the condom or to just pull out early and pray.

I was lonely for a friend. I longed for the secretive intimacy of my military man back home. I missed him but we were only able to talk for business reasons while I was deployed due to the official military communication channels. Tommy and I hardly communicated at all since he was putting together his own family and a life elsewhere. And I could talk to Lisa about some things, but I couldn't talk about our marriage and why it was a sham. I was not interested in hearing about her life on the base.

Get Here

It was not long after I got home from the deployment that I learned that there was a procedure and process to apply for special duty assignments. With the exception of my brief deployment to Riyadh, I had been stuck on base in Wyoming for five years at this point with no end in sight. I joined the military to see the world, not just the largest rodeo in America. If I was not going to get picked up for a regular assignment then I would force the system and apply for special duties in an effort to get me back to the east coast, where I felt the urge to be closer to my family. This was purely out of displaced romantic visions of a family life, not based in reality. By this time, Dad had remarried and had a new life, my brother barely spoke to Mom, and I would pick up right where I left off with Mom so many years before.

My marriage, understandably, was strained. I would do anything to avoid going home at night. I needed to keep busy in order to avoid thinking about the man on base. I volunteered, I worked on base long hours, and I held a second job at a convenience store around the corner. In between everything else, I did all the work required to manage the multiple rental properties Lisa and I had acquired. When I was home, I numbed my mind with alcohol. Avoid. Hide. Forget. Deny. Repeat.

I worked the system and navigated the special duty assignments until I landed an assignment in Springfield, Massachusetts. "Perfect," I thought to myself, "Just perfect." This gets us to the east coast and me closer to my troubled mom. When my mother and I spoke on the phone she was sounding increasingly depressed and lonely. I wanted to be there for her. My childhood may have had ups and downs with how I felt about my parents (what childhood doesn't?), but at this point, I was feeling like the only one who could ease my mother's burdens. I was hearing Oleta Adams's soulful ballad "Get Here" playing in the background of my mind. I would think to myself, "I am on my way, Mom, I am coming home to help."

Nor'easter Coming

I transferred with the Air Force to Massachusetts. We ended up living in Chicopee Falls, a favorite spot on the Mass Turnpike for my family and I to laugh about. (My family would roar at that name, "Where you going?" "I'm going to Chicopee Falls.")

Lisa and I were living on the base far away from her family and old friends from Ohio; even farther away from the newer friends she had made in Wyoming. We were starting over and Lisa was understandably lonely. She was relying on me for everything—to be her friend and her companion. I was feeling pressured, overwhelmed, anxious, and sad that I couldn't give her what she was seeking. She wanted children. Something to keep her busy. It made spending time at home more and more burdensome for me.

Meanwhile, my mother, just under two hours away over the Berkshire Mountains, in Albany, was going through her own metamorphosis. Her marriage to my dad had ended years ago like a dead limb of a giant oak tree finally falling to the ground during a blistering winter storm. Mom had left the restrictive Fundamentalist sect, rebooted her life, started going out to clubs, and was amusing herself in the social life of a big city. She began losing the weight that had piled on over the years as she stuffed feelings of insecurity down with food. She was coming into her own, coming out of the dark, if you will, and her joy from her newly found freedom was infectious. And just like I did as a child, I became an enabler for my mother, helping her live a decadent lifestyle.

As I drove from my current restrictive military routine life of rules, to my mother's new and vibrant life, I contemplated how very little had changed. I was still living dual lives. I was still hiding the real me from the neighbors and grandparents and acting like everything was fine when it really wasn't.

I would drive over the Berkshires to Mom's little townhouse, sometimes alone and sometimes with Lisa in tow, to melt into the comfort of Mom's strong arms, and bask in her warm, inviting smile and love. And just as I did as a child, I'd dream of how my life could be, if only I could be who I was on the inside, on the outside. Here I was, not THAT many years later, back in my mother's orbit, accepting her love and affection but not really having anything to do with my father. I didn't expect that my life would go back to watching *The Wonderful World of Disney* on television in footed pajamas as we did as kids, but I did feel like I was "home" and happy in those brief moments.

This new life of hers also found Mom surrounded by gays. The gays loved my mother, which I found odd as I assumed she would be praying hellfire and brimstone upon their sinful life choices. But I didn't care. I liked it. I felt at home, comfortable around these flamboyant widely extraverted, handsome men. They were older than me but damn funny. I still couldn't share my truth with these men, or my mother. How odd, I thought, that I was gay and worried about judgment all my life from my parents, and here was my mother embracing the gay men of the world as her posse. What bizarro world was I living in?

During my upbringing in the Fundamentalist religious sect, I was taught repeatedly that those living the lifestyle (being gay), would die a thousand slow deaths, and be met with fire and brimstone on the other side. I was NOT going to come out to anyone, especially my mother, and have her worry about my one-way ticket to hell. *Don't ask, don't tell.*

Seeing all the gays around my mom, living in their truth, started me on a downward slope into depression. Going home to a wife that I loved but felt nothing physical for, was sheer torture. But at this stage in my life, the happiness of moving back to the east coast that I had pined for when I was in Wyoming was not to be found. I became morbidly depressed and drank more and more. I was a rock star at work, but that was it; at home I was miserable, sad. Hell, I didn't even like being around me.

Yes, Mother

There was no doubt in anyone's mind that this boy was still a momma's boy. Mom and I spoke often on the phone, and I visited as much as I possibly could. One night while on the phone, my mother approached me directly, going in for the kill, asked me "Mark, is the reason why you are so unhappy and sad because you're gay?" Wait, what? We don't talk about anything serious—feelings, life, love, sex, sexuality. *Don't ask, don't tell.*

God, what a relief! I was so tired of having to decorate the dead moose in the living room in order to make it look like a coffee table! I could finally take my soiled sheets out of the closet and not be condemned or blamed. For the first time, my secrets weren't displayed to shame me. It was a liberating taste of openness. I drank it in because it was raw and real.

After a brief silence, like a spy giving out coded information, I looked around my basement laundry room to ensure the surroundings were clear to talk about the real "top secret information." I cleared my throat and whispered into the phone attached to the wall by the washing machine, "Yes, Mom, that is exactly the reason." I stopped breathing waiting to hear her response.

There was a long, silent, uncomfortable, pregnant pause on the phone. I cleared my throat, still waiting. She must have realized she had just accepted the lifelong briefcase of secrets I was now entrusting to her. You know the one, handcuffed and chained to your wrist? (Or maybe this one was being hauled around on my ankle like a ball and chain?) I had not foreseen coming out of the closet to family and friends until my mom had passed away and I was long out of the military. My relief quickly morphed into sheer panic.

I exhaled as Lisa came downstairs to bring me another cold beer. Phone calls with my mother would often last a long time. As Lisa shut the door at the top of the stairs, Mom finally came back with, "I love you, Mark, this is not going to be easy, but we are going to get through this, okay?"

Listening to me take a gulp of beer, knowing that the effects of alcohol combined with such raw emotions were a ticking bomb, Mom added, "It is so important that you stop drinking. Going through this now with alcohol in your system is so dangerous. You need a clear head, measured steps, and always remember to be balanced. What are you going to do next?"

Mom often talked to me about keeping balance in my life to help me control my manic type personality, for never letting up on myself which led to overachieving stress and exhaustion. During this most important conversation, the first time this GAY man was talking truthfully to his mother, she again began pitching the balance talk.

"You know how therapy has helped me get through everything over the last few years, right? I encourage you to see someone. It will help. Really!" She continued, "You have a lot of difficult work ahead of you. You need to stay balanced and keep it together to manage everything all at once."

"Uh huh," I agreed, non-committal. "I'll work on that."

"I want you to promise that you're going to stop drinking so much and start seeing a therapist. I'm not hanging up until you promise!"

"Okay, okay," I promised. "I have to find someone that I can speak to that isn't part of the military. I can't just blurt out everything. I need to figure all this out so it doesn't impact my career."

"I love you, Mark. We ARE going to get through this difficult time, one step at a time. Now get off the phone, stop drinking, and look into a counselor. Talk to you soon."

I sometimes think of my life at that time as three interlocked circles, like part of the Olympic Rings. In one circle, there's Happy-Go-Lucky Air Force Mark. In the second is Married Mark, where I was miserable and dying inside. And the third circle is Gay Mark: Hiding. Morbidly depressed. Needing Novocain to dull the pain.

With much trepidation, I acted on my promise to Mom, and I decided to go for counseling. I took precautions and went under an assumed name, Zach. I left my car, with the Department of Defense decal on the windshield, several blocks away from my gay therapist's office, so no one would know I was there.

The therapist was a young and handsome gay man. Tyler had worked with gay patients and their related issues before. He was understanding and wise in his ability to guide me without interfering with my individual process. I kind of liked it. I was able to openly talk about myself and for the first time, I didn't have to lie, cover-up, sneak, or change pronouns. It was comforting and comfortable. Talking to the therapist wasn't impacted by the fantasies that were whirling around in my mind about the therapist. I could have both, couldn't I?

In my half dozen or so sessions, I told my therapist, "I think I'm gay," but I really didn't unpack all my issues. I did tell him what happened with my mother during the "washing machine conversation." I told him about my marriage and the military. I focused on the pressure and stress of my situation within those parameters. He basically put my mind at ease.

Tyler shared information about support groups where married men with children were hiding their gay sexuality. My secret was that I was in the military and married, but Tyler said lots of gay people have many issues and hiding was not uncommon. Was the world filled with *Don't Ask, Don't Tell* people? I was relieved to know I was not alone, but sad to hear it was like an epidemic. How very sad.

Need-to-Know Basis

Back then the only way to really meet men was by going to the bars, getting set up by gay friends (which I didn't have), or answering or placing personal ads in the back of alternative local newspapers such as *Creative Loafing*. What an unbelievably scary set of options that was for a closeted military man. There was no way in hell I was sending a picture of myself in the mail to a total stranger. "It could be the private investigators for the Air Force," I thought with a small amount of paranoia. No amount of cockiness or boldness (or horny desires) could get me to gamble that amount of chance or risk. And, I kept reminding myself I was still MARRIED! To a woman. How could I be seeking a partner outside my marriage and still feel like I was living an ethical life? What about all that Christian learning? What about the military code of integrity? What about hurting Lisa—innocent and ignorant to all that I was going through?

I weighed whether or not I should tell my wife that I was gay. My wife was, after all, my best friend and this secret was hurting her. It hurt me more to know I was deceiving her. It hurt me that I couldn't share something so important about myself with her. I thought she MUST feel there was something I was hiding. I was growing so distant; putting space between her and the truth. But would telling her be for my benefit or for hers? Only later did I learn she was cheating on me the entire time we were married with other military men. I guess I was preoccupied keeping up with my own secrets.

My therapist intuitively asked whether Lisa really *needed* to know? Was it necessary to tell her in order to obtain a divorce? She was a lazy Catholic, only compliant when her mother was watching. Getting "permission" from her Catholic family was a likely obstacle to us finalizing a divorce. Would it make a difference at that point if I shared that I was gay?

If I shared my truth with her, would she be angry enough to cause trouble for me with the military? Would she jeopardize my career to exact revenge for keeping this a secret and marrying her in the first place? Would she be upset for "wasting" all that child-bearing time? Did she already know, way down deep? Could she feel my disconnection from our romantic life, even if I did rise to the occasion? Figuring out the best way to make this divorce happen would take some ingenuity.

I needed to ensure that Lisa didn't have a chance to ruin my career and that it was her choice to walk away. I needed to keep my secret but I also needed to set Lisa free, so she could have the life she deserved. Trying to give her what she wanted and knowing I would never be able to was torment-ing me.

An opportunity presented itself one night when Lisa went out with some of the ladies from the base. A plan came to me; bubbling up in little bursts from my slightly buzzed subconscious—each piece falling into place. I knew she had been drinking, and while we lived on base housing, if a depend-ent got a DUI, it was poorly reflected on the active duty member, and the dependent would lose driving privileges on base.

I did not like the ladies that Lisa hung out with. Some of them were less than desirable or respectable women, especially when their husbands were deployed or away from base. But I could not stop Lisa from associating with them from time to time.

This one particular night, I was having a few beers outside the row houses with some of the other husbands. When the ladies returned from their even-ing out, as they pulled up to the curb, one of the husbands made a comment, "Damn, I hope she was not drinking. They are really cracking down on DUIs on the base." When Lisa walked up the sidewalk to come into the house, I confronted her in front of her friends and the other husbands.

"Did you drive as drunk as you are? Why didn't you take a taxi? I can't believe you drove!" I challenged.

With liquid courage and peers to support her at that moment on the sidewalk, she replied, a little slur in her words, "Duh, how do you think I got home? You saw me pull up just now."

I hastily walked away and into our house, which was located in the middle of the row houses. As I walked away, the other husbands "Oohhed," and "Ahhhed," and one said, "Damn, she just put you in your place, Gibson!" "You better get control of your wife!" one of the other sergeants shouted to my back.

This was embarrassing and humiliating to me, as I was the military member and the wife was disrespecting and challenging me—almost to the point of belittling me. I slammed the door behind me imagining this signaled I was getting the last word or something. I went into the downstairs bathroom by the open window, so I could listen to the chatter outside. Lisa blew the whole incident off. "Ah, he will be okay. He is just bitchy tonight," she assured the ladies. None of these people, including Lisa, realized that this was all part of a bigger long-term strategy and they were all players in the show. I saw my opportunity to give Lisa what I knew she needed: freedom to start her life over. It wouldn't make me look good. It wouldn't be pretty. But I didn't know when I would get another chance.

As punishment for Lisa's total disrespect, I continued to get totally wasted and picked a fight with her, which drove her out of the house. Before she left, I threatened her loudly so the neighbors would hear, "Don't you walk out that door! If you do, that is the end!" I am sure she assumed this was just a drunken threat, or an ultimatum I would never enforce. She breezed by me in the hallway, "Get out of my way!" she screamed.

Hanging on the wall, next to the door, was a key holder with a pastoral nature scene painted on the top. Something we got at a craft fair, I think. We always put our keys on the hooks when we entered the house. When Lisa slammed the door shut in her haste to exit, the whole key holder crashed to the wood floor and all the keys to everything in our life scattered all over.

With the door locked behind her, I went downstairs in the basement, glanced over to the washing machine where I had divulged top secret information to my mother on the phone, and made my way to our toolbox. I was on a mission. I grabbed the hammer and a container of nails. Stomping back up the stairs, focused, no detours, I proceeded to nail the front door shut and repeated the same for the back door. Then I shut off all the lights and went to bed. Drunk as I was, I slipped easily into an almost comatose sleep.

A few hours later, a loud banging on the door woke me. My wife was back and appeared to still be drunk. I know I was. I got up and just sat on the floor at the top of the stairs in my boxer shorts and ignored the pounding, her crying, her pleas to open the door. Immobilized, I sat with my head in hands, tears in my eyes, knowing how this was hurting her, but could see no other choice but to stay motionless. I wanted to comfort my best friend and partner, but I wanted my deceptive life to be over. Tyler, my therapist, helped me realize that there is a life with relationships available for gay men. Why shouldn't Lisa have a life and relationship with a straight man? My biggest regret, to this day, is having brought Lisa into my world of perpetual secrecy.

At this point the neighbors were awake and peeking out from behind curtains or coming out their front doors. Soon after Lisa had gone, base security forces arrived and realized all was now quiet. They went away. I continued to remain upstairs and would slyly peek out the window between the cracks in the blinds and curtains. I could hear my testimony in my head, "I was drunk, sound asleep, and didn't hear a thing."

The next morning, like a trooper, I jumped out of bed, used the claw handle of the hammer to remove the nails in the door, showered, shaved, got into uniform, and scrambled out the front door to go to work. I could hear the nosy neighbor stirring next door as she got the kids ready for school. I had to pass by their kitchen window and front door to get to my car in the driveway. I made a B-line for the car and ignored her as she, dressed in her nightgown and bathrobe, tried to confront me as I backed down the drive.

I am sure the nosy neighbor alerted Lisa immediately. When I got to work, I instructed the front reception desk that I was not taking any personal phone calls during the test I was administering and instructed them to kindly take a message. I remember it was a Friday morning. Before leaving the house, I had packed a weekend bag and would depart for Albany directly from work.

Upon my return early Sunday evening, I found Lisa sitting in the dark in our living room. This would be the first time we would speak since "the incident," as I had successfully dodged her phone calls at work and all weekend. I acted like nothing was wrong. Because in *my* mind everything was right. I was going to free her from the agony of defeat and let her go from my crazy world. Now the trick was trying to figure out how to make her see this was for her benefit without disclosing my many secrets while maintaining my military career.

Lisa was extremely apologetic and tried really hard to make amends. Her pleas to keep us together tore me up inside. I told her calmly that it was over. I was going to pack a bag and go stay at a friend's house. A coworker at the MEPS, I told her, just so happened to need my help. I had been asked to watch my coworker's apartment, and take care of his cat, while he was on leave. She begged me not to go, but go I did.

This was actually perfect timing. During this break from Lisa and the artificiality of married life, I needed to figure out how I was going to navigate the next chapter of my life. Staying at a friend's home alone was probably the best thing I could do at the time. I could think clearly while no one knew where I was.

Toward the end of the two-week separation, Lisa did reach out to me and informed me that she did not want to live on base any longer. She said that the wives were all busybodies and getting on her nerves. Lisa proposed that she would move out temporarily in the form of a separation in order for us to attempt to work on our marriage. I agreed. She suggested counseling. I agreed.

What Lisa did not know is that I had already retained a lawyer, and he instructed me that I needed to proceed with a legal separation in order to start the waiting period time clock if I wanted the divorce. In our neck of the woods, one has to be legally separated for six months before filing for a divorce.

Lisa was not in tune to all the military rules, regulations, and jargon. She left that up to me. It was my career after all. I convinced her that legally in the eyes of the Air Force we had to have a legal separation in order for her to continue to receive benefits and health coverage. Lisa and I would start marriage counseling, but it didn't matter to me, as it was a façade designed to keep the clock ticking for the legal separation. I had to make it look like we had tried everything and we just could not reconcile. Lisa bought the legal separation concept for a little while, until those nosy housewives, I am sure, clued her in.

Suddenly I was served eviction papers from the first sergeant, as I was illegally living on base housing without my dependent. Lisa had notified the housing manager and first sergeant of the legal separation. I didn't see that one coming. There was definitely some embarrassment and shame being called out like that. Lisa had put my career and my record on the line. I was furious.

There was no turning back—especially when I learned she had retained a lawyer and all contact should be made between the attorneys until otherwise advised. Shit was getting real.

Closets are for Clothes

fter I separated from Lisa, I would travel back and forth to Albany to visit Mom. One particular weekend she was out of town but I decided to visit anyway. Now that I was out to Mom, I was on a mission. I wanted to experience a gay bar, and I felt safe being away from where I was stationed, but yet in my "home" community. Again, young and foolish, it never occurred to me to think about maybe running into someone I grew up with or even one of Mom's new gay friends and roommates! Alcohol blurred any sense of caution and reality!

My mom had a townhouse on South Pearl Street in downtown Albany, with secure parking out back. I remember having a couple of beers prior to calling a cab to take me uptown to the strip where the local gay bars were. Never having braved going to this part of town, I was nervous, but also confident in an odd way.

From the moment I walked into my first Albany gay bar, I felt comfortable. I had on my comfy tight jeans, so I felt like I looked good. The music was energizing and got my whole body buzzing. The bar vibe was alive and throbbing with the musk and pheromones of all sexually awake men. It was intoxicating and liberating.

I struck up a conversation with an older guy standing next to me. It was obvious to him that I was a gay bar "virgin." I told him that it was amazing to see guys dancing with guys and that I was in awe of how friendly everyone was. I turned to him and said, "I want that." Nothing in particular, I just wanted that feeling of acceptance to never go away.

Yes, we did end up leaving and going back to his apartment. Tom was an adjunct professor at State University of New York (SUNY) and really fit the part with his argyle socks, gray beret, and corduroy sports coat with leather elbow patches. I was working that fantasy of seducing a teacher and enjoying all the "education" I could gather!

Poor Tom. I poured my heart out to him explaining my plight—the military, my marriage, and my depression. Tom was kind, caring, and thoughtfully listened and provided objective advice. I was comforted to learn that there were others out there who had gone through the same thing. I was not as alone as I thought. I considered Tom my unofficial tour guide into the Land of Gaydom.

Later, I learned that Tom had a partner and that his partner was not as enamored with my unique military and divorce situation as Tom and I were. I just assumed everything was cool. When Tom told me that he had an open relationship with his partner and that it was common for gay couples to allow their partners to have sex with others, I believed him. But he had never told his partner about me. And having a relationship was not part of their deal. So once his partner found out about me, I had another secret to carry: I had to assure him that, "We're just friends."

I was in my element with having Tom in Albany during this tough time in my life. It was, after all, the name of the game for my life—shame and secrecy.

Out—and in the City

Never knowing how and where I would get the money (it somehow just always worked out), I developed the idealistic dream of living in the city. I wanted to be close enough to walk to work and near the nightlife that would allow me to explore being a newly single gay man.

I had been stationed at the Springfield Military Entrance Processing Station for several months when Brenda, my coworker, and I became close. Brenda was a mean, tough as nails marine. She was my trainer at the MEPS and provided on-the-job training. A typical Marine Corps figure, she was sharp in uniform, physically fit, and presented a badass persona. Some would fear her, which I would later learn she was okay with—especially since she was a shy, introverted person. I was hurting and I needed a confidant. Shortly after Lisa moved out, Brenda and I stopped at a bar next to the base one night after work. She had several beers and spilled her guts. She confided in me that she was asking her husband for a divorce and having an affair with a married officer. That was quite a secret—a career killer in the military.

Eventually I confided in her the miserable war zone behind the scenes of my otherwise picture-perfect life. I was happy, cheerful, motivated, reliable, and good at my job. No one would ever figure out that I was going through a personal hell in my private life. I shared with Brenda my pending divorce and the havoc that was playing with my finances, stress level, and work-life situation. I admitted that it was just how the cards were written. It felt good to talk to someone. I took comfort in her perspective. We were both exposed and vulnerable, but Brenda's secrets, at this point, were far worse and bigger than my own. Brenda was not cleared for my real top secret stuff—yet.

Brenda, originally from Boston, knew just how to navigate a big city. Having grown up in rural New York, then stationed in Cheyenne, Wyoming, I had no clue what to do in a city. I was far from street-smart. The thought of it scared the hell out of me. When people would stop me, I would talk to them and give them directions or whatever they asked for, but they all seemed to be asking for money. Brenda was not having it. She would double-time walk the streets and if someone tried to stop us or approach us, she would yell out, "It's 12 o'clock...it's always 12 o'clock!" Besides confusing me and the approaching person, I had no clue what she was doing. She later explained to me that, some homeless people and drug addicts try to stop you to get your attention because they are going to rob you. If you throw them off their game by blurting out it's 12 o'clock, it distracts them and you can keep walking. She thought my naivety was endearing and we burst out laughing. I still use this strategy today in Atlanta!

Knowing that my days living on the base were numbered, Brenda insisted I look at a few high-rise places within walking distance from our office downtown. I loved it! Freedom. I was on my own, as Patti LaBelle would sing. Brenda was also moving off base as she was sending her husband packing. She had another house about an hour away. She was not shy in telling me she wanted me downtown so she had a place to crash or stop over from time to time. I didn't mind, we quickly became like two misfit peas in a pod.

Emotionally, I had no one to talk to except my mother. Brenda knew about the divorce, which was bad enough in my mind, but not that I was gay—that was still code-word classified top secret. Even I knew that solely relying on my mother was not the healthiest of situations. Falling back into old patterns, my mother had once again buried her own emotions and put all the emphasis on me—and my struggle. The day she woke up and actually realized she had a gay son, I think she resented the fact that she never dealt with how she felt about it! Deep down, I knew it was a lot to process, as the Fundamentalist Christian cult sect would have me burned at the stake in town square at high noon. It would be difficult for her to find balance between her son and the lifelong teachings of religion. So, while Mom took some time away from me to process, a new level of excitement and distractions began in my world. Surprisingly, she did find a balance and advocated a new healthy lifestyle for me.

Don't Ask, Don't Tell

As I was making plans to move off the base into my new apartment, I learned through the work grapevine that there were a couple of "seedy" bars close to the office and my new apartment downtown. "It's a gay bar," my coworkers confided in whispers. I laughed to myself and thought, "How did they know?" Turns out some of the civilian girls would go to the bars to dance as they proclaimed, "They (the gay bars) are great, there's never a line for the ladies' room."

I remember feeling cocky and bold as I went to a gay bar so close to where I worked. After all, I worked in the part of the military where I met all the new recruits. But getting ready to be free of my wife had emboldened me to go beyond sensible behavior.

This newfound freedom was colliding with big news out of another house—the White House.

I remember sitting at my desk in a mostly glass office that looked out over Main Street. The breaking news that morning was that President Clinton just signed a new bill into law—the Don't Ask, Don't Tell (DADT) policy. CNN went on to explain the "highlights" of the policy which would allow closeted members of the military to serve, while prohibiting those who were openly gay from military service. The shared office was typically abuzz, but during this announcement it came to a silent halt, everyone frozen, staring at the TV. After the breaking news, I turned back toward the window and put my hands on the keyboard, my shoulders sank, and my eyes closed. I suddenly felt a sense of relief because superiors could not ask military members about their sexual orientation. But this false sense of relief quickly diminished to sheer panic as I slipped into an almost trance-like state, trying to process the news, confused as to why the United States Military would encourage anyone to reject their true authentic self by enacting a law. The irony of the Army's recruiting slogan, "Be all you can be," was not lost on me in that moment.

Luckily for me, I had an Air Force active duty supervisor at the MEPS (who would go on to earn the title as the Best Boss in the Air Force years later), come up behind me, put his giant strong hand on my shoulder and gave it a squeeze, "Mark, you okay? The phone is for you." Startled, I replied, "Oh, um…I am fine—just need coffee or something. Let me grab the phone, thanks." And just like that, I was on another routine phone call.

Bright Lights—Big City

The gay bar down the street piqued my curiosity. I met a man within seconds of walking into that whispered about, forbidden bar. It was a bar for guys in their forties or older, so I was one of the youngest guys in the joint. The place was dark and filled with smoke swirling around in the rays of the few can lights in the ceiling. I was suddenly uneasy as I made my way to the bar. "What'll you have, sexy?" the bartender asked seductively. Embarrassed, I bashfully ordered a beer. Familiar with the bartender, this handsome, macho guy, who was much closer to my age, came up next to me at the bar, chastised the bartender to stop embarrassing me and then turned and introduced himself to me, "Hi, I'm Joe." It was obvious I was nervous. But, I couldn't stop smiling, as I shook his hand and introduced myself.

The group of guys surrounding us got larger as Joe introduced me to everyone. I was more attracted to Joe's confidence and relaxed attitude than anything physical at first. He took me under his wing. He had striking, deep, dark eyes, a fun, bashful laugh, and dark, wavy hair. It didn't take long before we agreed it was time to get out of there. We were far too young, so was the night.

Joe took to me to a wild dance club a few blocks over. This place was NYC Studio-54 kind of wild! The music was loud, the bass was thumping, and everyone was bumping; the lights were pop bulb flashing alternating with laser neon light swords; the go-go boys in jock straps were dancing on tall blocks sporadically scattered around this huge club like provocative gods in the sky looking down on their minions. My jaw dropped to the floor in amazement. I was in awe—or in Oz—I didn't know which, but I knew it was out-of-this-world fantastic.

Joe seemed to know everyone, and I enjoyed being fawned over as he introduced me to all his friends. After each time, he disappeared to "use the bathroom," he became more bold and physical with me.

Joe and I would delve into a wildly intense physical affair. But before I officially moved off base, before I moved downtown, I turned up the charm and danced my way into Joe's apartment where I would stay for hours to escape. One day, he saw my Air Force cap in the car and started telling people I was in the military. I shut that down real quick!

For several weeks, we had a wild, passionate affair: in elevators, parking garages, anywhere with the element of surprise. It was an awesome rush, almost getting caught when he kissed me as the elevator doors would open and so on—almost to the point where it would push me over the edge to punish myself, later drowning in alcohol for being so careless and stupid.

I worked the later shift and typically arrived at work at 2 p.m. One afternoon I came rushing into the office with my usual exuberance and found the commander there. Everyone was standing at attention, so I moved quickly and grabbed a spot on the wall behind the door. When the meeting concluded, before the commander left, she nonchalantly and rhetorically asked, while walking and peering over her shoulder at me, "I wonder why I saw Sergeant Gibson standing outside a gay bar over the weekend?" And then she walked out. I wanted to jump under the desk! I thought for sure that my entire military career was going to be over—the jig was up. I wanted to puke. I began freaking out. That was the commander's way of saying that she knew. My coworkers remained quiet. Brenda was horrified.

However, she could not ask, and I was not telling.

The Nixon era had deemed that gays in the military or government were lacking in integrity, proclaiming we were unfit for duty because this character flaw would make us easy prey to bribes. Here I was, trusted with a secret security clearance and a private life that I had managed to keep top secret.

But we couldn't keep a secret?

Bitch, please!

On the Rocks

When I was ready to cart my belongings out of base housing, I solicited the assistance of my newfound distraction to help me. Joe rallied a posse of gays to come to the base and help me move. Brenda helped me secure a gorgeous apartment downtown (the Gucci standard for apartments in Springfield) within walking distance of the office. Freedom! I relished the air and funky vibe of my new one-bedroom, loft apartment. There was always plenty of beer and loud music to drown out any emotional problems that might exist. I began to dabble in learning how to cook, changing from a strict meat and potatoes kind of guy to reading and practicing *Bon Appétit* menus on my friends. Brenda was a foodie, and it was the common ground for us to talk food when we weren't sharing our secret lives of misery and hell.

At this point, drained of energy, pickled with alcohol, I decided I needed a mini-vacation. The fight was on with Lisa for the properties we owned together. My divorce proceedings were getting heated with lawyer's fees accumulating exponentially, and that, combined with the move off the base and the gossip of the neighbors, was stressing me out. I wanted to shut it all off and escape! So I made reservations.

Again, bold and unquestionably in denial, I decided to take Joe, my gay LOVER, to a military resort called Fourth Cliff on the Outer Banks coast of Massachusetts, near the Cape. Fourth Cliff had R&R cabins for military use only—rented through Hanscom Air Force Base in northeastern

Massachusetts. Looking back, I can't believe I could be so cavalier as to take my gay lover to this place, but I did.

There was an inexplicable force pulling me there, or maybe I was living in a parallel universe! Perhaps it was the call of blissful, peaceful, hassle-free summers of childhood fun with my family on Cape Cod that enticed me back to the beach. The ocean was like the effervescent noise you hear when you open a soda.

In any case, flaunting my sexuality in a military setting just added to the denial and messy tangled web of secrecy my life had become. Despite my promises to myself to improve my behavior, my life continued on in this manner. I was getting really, really good at living so close to the edge. Like riding in the front car of a roller coaster, but with no seatbelts or harness to lock you in place. There's a chance that I needed to be on a high wire, with the risk of falling, the risk of being injured, as the only ways to be sure I was still alive.

As Joe and I went through the gate check-in and security, I told them I was with my "cousin." As we headed up the familiar drive toward the check-in office, I asked myself why the hell would I add this much chance or potential volatility to my sacred, peaceful place? I would retreat here often as the water had a calming effect. Here I could get centered, feel balanced, and feel tranquil. Why potentially ruin my only escape from the madness of my life? Of course, I had no logical answer.

Bud, an older retired fella, former military, worked the front desk. He always offered a welcoming smile accompanied with nosiness to get all up in my business. He would not have approved of my secret getaway weekend plans for sure. But I was far too quick-witted for the likes of Bud. I would fire back snappy responses to his inquisitive investigation about the man in the car that was waiting for me. Bud was trying to discern my "intentions." I had an iron-clad, well-rehearsed scenario in my mind. No retired military guy was going to figure out *my situation*! Even then I am sure I laughed at myself thinking how stupid, "Yeah, right. Kissing cousins staying in a cottage for the weekend."

All in all, Joe and I spent a nice, long weekend without incident—relaxing, drinking, reveling in the wildness of it all, and appreciating the ocean view. We took late night walks on the beach. The rejuvenating sounds of the ocean at Fourth Cliff were just what I needed. I propped the windows open to hear the calming whispers of the ocean waves crashing against the rocks below. I slept soundly.

It was Sunday morning, time to check-out. We were about to leave, Joe was still inside, and Bud hollered out to me as I was loading the car, "When are you planning on paying your phone bill?" he asked.

"We haven't made any calls," I told him.

"I can assure you that you have made quite a few calls," he admonished. "I can show you the print out."

"No problem" I responded. "I'll come to the office in a few minutes. Thanks, Bud!" I threw up a friendly wave.

While Joe was in the shower, I headed for the office. I was shocked, not only to see the frequent amount of calls (apparently made every time I left the cabin or ran to the store for supplies, based on the time stamps), but especially, when looking at the same number called repeatedly, I knew that the phone number looked familiar—it belonged to my wife!

Feeling a rush of emotions I calmly said, "Oh, I'm sorry, Bud. My cousin must have made those calls. How much do I owe you?" I paid the $11.73.

Walking back to the room, I was out of my head horrified. The complete and utter betrayal! I had to keep it together while I was still on a military installation, I warned myself. But I was seething inside; I could only see red! I went into self-defense mode. I wanted to understand the entire story, and THEN I would figure out what to do about it. Back at the cabin, Joe was out of the shower, naked and waiting for some fun with me on the bed. I needed to be smart about this. I wanted answers but didn't want to risk my career! Patience. Breathe. Think. I would get the truth out of him one way or another.

I replied to Joe's romantic post-shower advances with a sharp command, "Get dressed. We have to go. It's past checkout time." I went into the bathroom shut the door and splashed my face with cold water and held my face in my hands, "Think, Mark, think."

I finished loading the car with the last few things as Joe scampered to the car, making light conversation and chit chat, trying to be all coy with me. I wanted to punch him in the face, followed by yelling a resounding WTF, but I kept it together. While we were driving, my mind was racing. I wasn't really focused on anything he was saying as he fidgeted in the seat and adjusted the radio. "Never any Goddamn stations this close to the water," he chanted.

Why would Joe be calling my wife? How did Joe even know my wife? Why was this a secret? What was he hiding from me? Didn't he know there would be charges on the phone that I would know about? He didn't even ask me about paying for the calls as we left the property. Did he *want* me to know something? Did he *want* me to ask him about the calls? Enraged, my mind raced faster than a NASCAR driver.

When we were finally on the Mass Pike I announced that I needed to stop for gas. Joe said he had to use the bathroom. Before pulling off the highway, I gave Joe a chance. "Please tell me the truth," I pleaded to him in my head.

"Joe, I am only going to ask you this once. Don't lie to me."

"What's wrong, Mark?" He asked in a caring tone.

"Did you call my wife over the weekend?"

He laughed and said, "No, why would I do that?"

"No reason," I laughed and pretended to shrug it off.

"Busted, asshole. You are so busted," I thought to myself, as the full force of the Scorpio birth sign was about to retaliate.

I took the rest stop exit. We parked for gas and he made a motion to grab my ass. Public displays of affection were totally out of the question, and he knew it, but tried to push the limits all the time. As I watched him walk away, turn back, and wink at me provocatively. I left him, his bags, and our torrid affair on the Mass Pike where my soon-to-be ex-wife could retrieve them all!

"No wonder Lisa seemed to be able to anticipate my every move in the divorce proceedings," I mused as I drove back to Springfield alone. Joe must have been telling her everything under the guise of being my friend. Because of all the real estate we mutually owned, Lisa stood to gain a considerable amount in the divorce. I thought I was being kind and helping Lisa move on in a positive way with someone she could love. What was she doing with Joe? Was Joe sleeping with both of us? I was NOT going to lose all the income properties because of a man that betrayed me! It was on now, the gloves were off. I called my attorney.

A few weeks later, one afternoon at work, Joe called me, wanting to reconcile. I wasn't really interested, but wanting to keep my enemy's closer, acquiesced to a meeting. We talked about nothing memorable and, oddly, he gave me a gift bag as we said goodbye. When I got home, I looked inside. Edible panties and a dildo? Obviously, he got his gift bags mixed up. I could only imagine what my wife found in hers! What an idiot.

There was not enough beer in the world to help numb this wild-ass chapter in my life, where my gay lover was also dating my soon-to-be ex-wife. Jerry Springer anyone?

Turning Tables

L isa asked to meet with me, yet again, to talk about additional changes to the details of our divorce. This tactic of needing to change a paragraph, a sentence, something, over and over, was getting tiresome. I was paying for the divorce and all the lawyer's fees were adding up. Every time Lisa made a change, it needed to be resubmitted and thus would increase the billable hours for the attorney. Every time we came to an agreement, she would find fault with it. So here we were, having a drink at a quaint little eatery, not far from my new, fabulous, downtown bachelor pad, and not far from my office. (She was pissed that I would not tell her where I was living.) What would it be this time? I wondered as I finished off my second beer before she arrived.

She looked fantastic! She had her hair and makeup done, and was dressed in new clothes. She certainly turned a few heads as she walked toward me. She was overconfident and bubbly—but she didn't fool me, I knew something was up. Probably more changes to the divorce documents that I would have to pay for. Or maybe she was trying to manipulate me by looking— with the exception of her shoes—fabulous? Didn't she know I was gay and that her coy ways would not have any effect on me? Did Joe tell her my secret?

The initial casual conversation quickly dissolved into the usual nasty disagreements. She abruptly pulled out a trump card when she saw I wasn't giving in.

"I'll tell the military your *secrets*. You'll lose everything," she said smugly.

I was freaking out. I had no idea what she knew or didn't know at this point. Or, was it just a bluff? Was she fishing for information? Joe could not have anything to gain if he told her about the sexual affair he and I were having. Would he? I panicked.

"Really?" I replied. "Then we'll stay married forever, for the rest of our lives." I said with wild, angry, sullen eyes.

"I LOVE youuuuuu," sarcasm dripping from my exaggerated enthusiasm. I smiled at her viciously.

"You son of a bitch!" She snarled, flipping the table over and my beer in my face!

"And I'll tell your mother about the affair you're having," I continued, as the beer dripped from my hair down my face, soaking the front of my shirt.

I went on, sarcastically, arms gesticulating with overly dramatic big, loving embraces, "We were young. We just hit a bad patch in our marriage like all young couples do, honey. No, we'll work this out. Wait, stop, please. I LOVE you!"

I knew she had to save face with her devoutly Catholic mother and to do so, I would have to remain the villain. But if I shed some light on her not-so-perfect lifestyle, I could turn the tables. I needed to manipulate my wife to make her see that it just was not going to work out.

"Just sign the Goddamn papers," I urged her. "Be free of me and the properties. Go and start your new life with your new boyfriend."

In the end, my attorney was ruthless once he was armed with the new information that Lisa was having an affair, and that I was willing to reconcile. I never let on that I knew it was Joe. My attorney told Lisa's attorney the make and model of the car and the license plate number and assured her that it would not be long before we learned her lover's name.

She became nervous or tired or both, and eventually she'd buy the bluff. But after the table-flipping and public humiliation, I was angry. I drove to my attorney's office, marched in, and interrupted a meeting he was having. I told him to unleash the dog. Game over. He knew exactly what to do next.

If she would have just signed the divorce papers earlier, Lisa would have gotten half of everything (including the properties), and I would have managed the majority of the marital debt. But that ended up being a very expensive beer for her to splash in my face! VERY expensive.

My attorney ended up suing Lisa for all legal fees. We split the marital debt, and I walked away with ALL of the properties we amassed during the marriage. My attorney sued her for palimony until the martial debts were settled. Even I thought that was a bit over the top.

Eventually, Lisa pleaded with me that she just wanted a clean break after she heard how incredibly complicated I would make her life, or remain "in love." Soon after, I was officially divorced.

It was not until after the divorce settlement, while we were dividing and exchanging the remaining Christmas decorations from her family that Lisa had left behind, that I met with her in person. When I saw her that last time, she looked great. I felt a sense of relief that she would be just fine over time. As we said goodbye I knew I would never see her again. But before she could leave, I told her to be careful with Joe, that I did not trust him. We both knew what I meant. She knew I had figured out she was having an affair with Joe, who had once been my gay lover. In the end I learned that she did, in fact, marry him and have children. So sad, I thought to myself. I had inherited enough Polish/Catholic traits to assume responsibility and guilt for ruining Lisa's life. Friends, family, and therapists assured me I was no longer responsible for her choices in life, but still.

Testing 1-2-3

In spite of my marriage ending and rounding the corner on the problems my homosexuality exploration caused in my life, my assignment to the Springfield MEPS was exciting. I had an edge or leg up on my joint service counterparts. I was one of a few Air Force representatives and remained upbeat, positive, and motivated. Years later coworkers were shocked and horrified to learn I was going through so much turmoil, but still kept it together. Boastful pride rang out in my head. "Yeah, that's how I roll!" I would think to myself, "I am fine" as I would thank them for their kindness and thoughtfulness.

The job itself was a tedious and thankless job with nothing creative to keep one interested. But the one constant was the professionalism of the military members who were assigned there; a cross-section of each service. I was proud to represent the Air Force.

My direct supervisor at the time was undoubtedly one of the best supervisors I had throughout my entire military career (officer or enlisted). He was an unexcitable sergeant, looked sharp in his uniform, and was a strong leader. Because I was loud and over-the-top positive, people would continually come after me or try to burst my bubble, to bring me down. As long as I continued to do a great job and excel, I made the whole department look good. I think it was almost a full-time job for my supervisor to run top cover and protect me from the negative forces out to get me. Misery loved company and I was a total threat to those who were miserable.

In the office, I knew that he could tell I was going through a lot in my personal life. From time to time, he would place his strong, large, powerful hand on my shoulder—give it a squeeze and ask, "Are you okay?" That was as touchy or feely as you were ever going to get out of this tough sergeant who never cracked a smile. But it meant so much to me, those few words and gestures of kindness. He guided me and made sure I stayed within the boundaries at work. Luckily for him, I was a good airman with bountiful positive energy, regardless of what was going on in my living hell of a personal life.

Secrets and Snowflakes

Shortly after my divorce, I began a wild friendship with Brenda AND the married officer with whom she was having a torrid affair. This was right up my alley. Clandestine, covert operations were my life! Guarded words, eye-contact messages, knowing grins and smiles, nods—we just needed a secret signal (like the nose flick used in *The Sting* to signify the beginning of the con) to make the drama complete. All the while, we were never unprofessional in public. Actually, we were never seen together in public or went anywhere we might encounter any other military personnel.

Brenda's lover was Latino. I was not well versed in cultural stereotypes and didn't know that Latino lovers were supposedly passionate and over the top in intensity, possessiveness, control, and jealousy. But like a predator he could see her weaknesses, swept Brenda off her feet, and made her feel incredible!

Their relationship, such as it was, was marred with much drama. But the good times were great. Brenda bought his perpetual promise of leaving the good-for-nothing wife—hook, line, and sinker. He lavished her (and me, for that matter) with elaborate gifts, limo rides, a taste of high society—but underground, if that makes sense. My secrets were safe as long as those two could maintain their relationship. Brenda was another person caught in the trap of living an alternate life, one that was not her true self. She could never share her real self, because there were too many secrets hidden. I often wondered if Brenda and I would have been friends had we not had so much dirt on each other? If we were both clean and clear, what would our lives have looked like? Our lungs and livers would have been healthier, that's for sure.

As I was getting ready to depart MEPS for my next assignment, I was also preparing to leave Brenda and her Latin lover behind. I was also training my replacement. His name was Mike, and he was a model airman.

Brenda had a house near a ski resort, about an hour away. Since we all had a long weekend coming up from work, a group of us were heading out there for a weekend. It was snowing like a scene in a snow globe as we cheerily, and drunkenly, drove out to what would later be dubbed "Margaritaville" (a juxtaposition for the blizzard upon us.) We were talking and laughing and suddenly walking through accumulated snow on the pristine white driveway of Margaritaville. As Brenda's divorce was final and her husband had moved out, there was no one to shovel the driveway in preparation for our arrival.

Trudging through the near knee-deep snow with luggage and liquor, Brenda made a remark to our small group about how she and the married officer were having an affair. I was in shock. *What the hell was she doing?* I remained focused on not falling on my ass while carrying all the booze. Without skipping a beat, Mike surprised and in disbelief, laughed saying, "The next thing you're going to tell me is that Mark is gay." I wanted to jump into the water of secret telling too. I blurted out, "I am!"

SHOCKER! *That* was an interesting weekend. It was the first time I had come out to anyone in the military! Mike's wife was European—nonchalant and accepting, she didn't understand the complexity of it all, which was, in itself, refreshing. Mike was fully aware of the complexity and difficulty this secret would be for us. He assured me it was not a big deal, but he also knew it was a difficult and sensitive situation. We remain friends to this day.

Rules of Engagement

Brenda was the first confidant I had in the military who knew that I was gay. When she needed someone to act as her husband or boyfriend for "plus one" events, business or family gatherings, and because her real partner was actually married to someone else, I was her cover boy—her beard. And vice versa—we totally played up on this scenario. It was a win-win situation, except she expected a lot of me as a "spouse" and as a friend. She kept my confidence, as long as I helped her keep her secret.

Her officer lover knew my divorce story. Eventually he did find out about my being gay, and it did not faze him. Why would it? His penalty would have been far worse if I told his secret; he could have gone to jail! It was ideal for him, actually—a male friend spending so much time with his mistress so that everyone thought we were having an affair: "Mark is gay and I am the one actually having the affair, but we can blame it on Mark," must have been his thinking. They both would have been discharged if they'd been caught. The whole thing was dangerous, playing with fire—wild! Secretly, I didn't mind this complicated mess, because I was sipping the nectar of freedom for the first time. Here were people actually knowing me, and I was okay, they were okay. But we were all hiding behind lies and deception. I just accepted, as I had always done, that this was how life was going to be and the price one would have to pay.

It felt natural to live this way, since I had spent all my youth living just like this! My lack of self-worth fed into the idea that I had to provide something, some benefit, for anyone to like me. I was only valued when I subverted my true self to allow someone else to rise. I would bask in the ideas or relish the thoughts of what it must have felt like to be on the other side, the "more thans" versus the "less thans."

I pushed family and potential friends away, because the idea that I couldn't let anyone into my secret life unless I had leverage on them was ingrained into my consciousness. I was in a vicious cycle that was my new norm in dealing with my sexuality and career.

My relationship with Brenda became more about control and manipulation. In the end, after many years of on again and off again times in each other's lives, our relationship in that form could not withstand the test of time. As I came more into my own truth and was able to be honest with myself about what I wanted—what I deserved—I was finally able to stand up for myself, and then Brenda found no value in having me in her life.

Who's Foolin' Who?

Closer to home, I learned that my mom's boyfriend, a former class-mate of my brother, was being booted from the Navy for drug use. At first, I truly believed the stories that he was framed and the drugs were planted on the ship. I also believed the stories that the relationship with my mother was just a pen pal type relationship while the guy was in the Brig (Navy prison).

The boyfriend eventually found his way to Mom's house after being released from the Brig, and it was only then that I finally deduced that it was more than a pen-pal relationship. I never asked, my mom never told! It just was.

I began to secretly despise the entire situation and this man. Every time this low-life sold my mother a new story about another scuffle with the law, a loss of a job, or how someone had wronged him, she in turn would repack-age the story and pitch it to me and my brother with some syrupy What Would Jesus Do type of absurd disingenuousness. Outwardly, to my mother, I approved of this derelict, since—selfishly—this was definitely distracting her from my situation. What was sickening to watch was the epic big-screen movie Mother was writing to enhance the drama in her own life. I kept the smoke blowing in the air, because it kept everyone redirected to Mom's drama, and that worked quite nicely for me. Deflect, deflect, deflect.

After the drug addict's bullshit stories ran their course, my mother finally broke it off only to find herself in repeated affairs with married men—each one needing her to fix them more than the last. With none of them ever leaving their wives as promised.

Good Fortune

In one of the most dramatic times of my life, Brenda, my military counterpart and confidant, was having an affair with a married officer, I was a closeted gay man and in the military, my mother was dating a convict/drug addict/con man, and I had been in the middle of a divorce while having a relationship with a man who turned out to be sleeping with my soon-to-be ex-wife.

As if my life didn't already have enough drama, I was dragged off to visit a fortune-teller in Springfield by a new work friend, Ann, a travel agent. Ann was gorgeous and vivacious. She was smart, funny, and loved her job as a civilian contractor charged with getting new recruits on planes, trains, and automobiles to their prospective boot camps.

Ann went to a fortune-teller regularly and claimed that everything foretold had always come to pass. I didn't believe in this loosey-goosey stuff, but it was something new to try, so I went along with the group. I especially knew it was taboo and flew in the face of the Fundamentalist religion introduced to my youthful, developing self so many years before.

After the fortune-teller visit, we went out to a bar. We were all comparing notes. My "fortune" was so outlandish that I felt like I got ripped off. The fortuneteller said I was going to change careers, go off to a distant world, become like Mother Theresa, saving children in a village, and that I would obtain multiple higher education degrees. I was pissed and wanted my money back! We would all laugh as we ordered another round of drinks. She hadn't come up with anything that sounded remotely probable or even reasonable. I was in the military all the way, didn't like school and wasn't planning on going back, and didn't think I would be traveling much more than where the Air Force sent me. It was entertaining at best and my visit enabled the group to get a discount, so be it.

Now, I wish I had kept the paper she gave me with my fortune. Everything that fortune-teller predicted back then, gradually came true over the next few years. Now if she only gave me a series of winning numbers, right?

Listening to a prediction of my future by the fortune-teller made me realize how much I had hidden in the past. The future as she foretold it sounded so dignified, even noteworthy. This was a life that somebody else lives, the "more thans," not me, I thought. My burden made me feel that I was not even good enough to remain in the life I had.

Whirling Dervish

After my time with MEPS in Springfield, I was either going back to the mainstream Air Force or I had to find another special duty assignment if I didn't want to go back to a base. I learned of a potential opening right up the road from Springfield in Worcester, closer to Boston. The opening was at the ROTC (Reserve Officer Training Corp) detachment located at Worcester Polytechnic Institute. I interviewed and knew that I nailed the interview. (It was just a feeling that I became familiar with deep down inside—I could feel it in my bones.) I went back to Springfield to pack up my apartment. I knew I got the job. I had never in my wildest dreams figured on how this one interview and assignment would change the course of my military career—and life—forever.

Worcester Polytechnic Institute was a school for very intelligent folks and it was very expensive. It is not easy to get accepted to their program; even more challenging to stick to and complete the program. I was honored to be on campus. It was a classic New England picture-book place. Ivy-covered walls, old, red-brick buildings, four seasons of greenery to enjoy with lots of trees and grass. And when you walked the hallways, you got a whiff of that old book smell that makes you feel like you're becoming part of history.

The leadership team at the unit was phenomenal. Everyone was high speed. I was up for the challenge to raise the bar. I completely enjoyed working there as a staff sergeant and thought of this as a new chapter in my life, as closeted as it was. I was surrounded by academia and stellar professors. My role was to support them administratively and functionally. It didn't take me long to get bitten by the academia bug. It had taken me years and years up to this point to complete a few college-level courses. I was not the smartest egg in the dozen, but I had passion and drive that, once focused, would be unstoppable.

Out of the blue, I decided to make an appointment with a counselor at the local state college. Worcester was such an amazing city. On the way into Worcester from the highway, I noticed a billboard which read, "The greatest cities in America have a college; Worcester has ten."

I drove across town to meet with a counselor during a lunch break. Even though I was in uniform, I was timid about pursuing school. The counselor got up from her desk and ushered me out her door. She said, "C'mon, go for a walk with me."

As we walked, we got to the bottom of why I thought it was taking so long to get a degree. Did I even want a degree? I was brutally honest with her. I told her, "Ma'am, I can't do math." She grabbed my arm, causing me to stop and look right into her eyes. She said "Is that it? Is that the only reason?" I nodded and said "Yes," as if I let her in on one of my biggest secrets. (There were plenty more where that came from, I thought to myself…not liking math was nothing in comparison.)

As we continued to walk, we soon came upon an impressive red brick, New England-style building on the campus. We marched right into the communications building and landed at the director's office. "I want you to meet Staff Sergeant Mark Gibson. He is going to enroll here and I think he is your next superstar in Communications. Can we assure him that no math is allowed?" The director threw the book he was reading from his desk to the floor as a sign of solidarity and distaste for math as well, and said, "Hell NO, absolutely, no math allowed. Classes start in two weeks, meet me here at 2 p.m."

I learned of a program that allowed a two-year break in your military time commitment to pursue a degree. If the military had a need for a certain skill, and you went out on your own to earn the degree, you could return to the military and get a commission as an officer.

The governor of Massachusetts created a policy in which tuition at a state school would be waived for active military or veterans. This made it more affordable for me to attend college, as my pay would be suspended during my educational break from military service.

The tuition waiver was a sign of sorts. Excited, I realized *this* was it! My next overachieving goal in life. But this time, it was JUST ALL ABOUT ME.

When you start a new job, the military had an unwritten rule that you were not allowed to enroll in evening classes until you were proficient in your duties; it was typically a one-year waiting period. Everything can be waived in the military. I was able to convince my commander to let me start taking a class at night. To him a class was one, not four. This was an incredible workload plus a new job. I was used to a double life; this time I was at least using my duality skills in favoring myself versus the self-destructive life I had been living.

Luckily, I had listened to my dad years before when he strongly, I mean STRONGLY, encouraged me to sign up for the GI Bill in boot camp. You only got one shot to sign up and you had to have $100 deducted from your pay for the first year. "Dang," I thought at the time, "That was a lot of beer money." And here I was, ten years later, so glad I skipped those beers—even though there were plenty of others I didn't skip!

My master plan was to attend a state school for my bachelor's degree—using the GI Bill as a stipend to offset living expenses. I decided that I wanted it all and I wanted it all at the same time. I only had a two-year break from active duty. I got my draft plan together and made another appointment to meet with the counselor to ensure she was on board and we could make it happen.

She was the key to my success, she unlocked so many doors for me and was my cheerleader. Because of her, I managed to receive unusual permission from the state board of education and board of regents (long story) to simultaneously go for my bachelor's AND master's degrees. And, not to be bored (ha ha), I would get both of these degrees while I was also going to ROTC! For this, I was committed to providing four years of service to the military post-graduation. I was ready for a break from the tedium of administrative duty.

While I was at ROTC, I got a great apartment in an area of town called Crown Hill. The community was fully accepting of diverse lifestyles. I met the gay couple next door and felt immediately welcomed and comfortable. The community was super proud to have a military man in the neighborhood. I was invited to many events and parties. There were progressive cocktail parties that helped me meet lots of my neighbors.

My quaint and charming apartment was in the servant quarters building in back of a huge Victorian house. Mary, an older woman with lots of energy, lived up front in the mansion and kept a watchful eye. Mary was supportive of everything I tried and did. There wasn't ever a discussion; it was understood. Everything that I did, Mary attended. All of my schooling successes were praised and recognized.

I went to Worcester State College for a bachelor's degree in Communications during the day, Worcester Polytechnic Institute for Air Force ROTC studies some days, some weekends, and then Clark University for my master's degree in the evenings.

While I was going to all these classes and completing the course work, I had to complete an internship in order to graduate with the master's program.

The Power of Radio

I was short eight credit hours for completion of my master's degree, and my advisor and I began developing an internship plan/idea. A Crown Hill neighbor (I was working those connections) was able to get me an interview at Bose Corporation. All I needed was a foot in the door to pitch an internship idea/concept. The internship would give me additional college credits and required me to be there for twenty hours a week. Though I was getting my schooling paid for and a small stipend, I was technically not on duty, so, I was no longer receiving a paycheck. I needed money to live! When was I going to fit in a job?

As fortune would have it, my new intern supervisor at Bose, Cindy, said they were having trouble getting the application approved through HR because I needed to be hired as an entry-level employee due to insurance requirements. So she told me the only way my internship would work was if they could pay me. They "hired" me in an entry-level position, with intern credit for school. My internship was to help analyze and recommend changes to their phone sales calls for the new Bose Wave Radio.

After hours and hours of listening to recordings of incoming calls and sitting next to sales people making calls, I was able to format my own sales pitch. I suggested that I try it out for a while to see if it worked. It worked! I was doing so well, that I became the #2 salesperson in the company that first year—and I was only part-time and an intern.

By the end of the second year, my internship was complete, and I had become the #1 salesperson. I was offered a full-time job for in-bound marketing if I thought the military wasn't the direction for me.

Truthfully, part of my success was all the publicity that the newly-launched radio got, but the rest was pure bluster and enthusiasm and becoming practiced at telling a story that the listener wanted to hear. I was closing nine out of ten calls. In fact, I needed help to wrap up the sales, so I could move on to the next caller!

Cindy and I rewrote sales training manuals using my closing formula chatter, and the whole company was making tons of sales. And, to boot, I earned more money working part-time at an internship than I was earning working full-time as a staff sergeant in the Air Force!

Spinning Spokes and Plates

Not content to rest on those laurels, while I was at Bose and going for my bachelor's degree and studying for my master's degree, I was a cadet in the ROTC program doing aerospace studies. During this time, I was nominated to be the Cadet Wing Commander of the ROTC Cadet Corps. I was responsible for all the other cadets! This was in addition to drill time, physical fitness, uniform preparation, undergoing inspections, and so on. Molding a new officer was a rigorous program.

No matter what I did, no matter how many responsibilities I had, I always found ways to send money home to my mother. I bought her a car at auction. Yes, another car. And I would visit her in Albany. I didn't neglect my family, despite the heavy study and workload I was committed to completing.

Dad called me somewhere in the middle of the two intense years to ask me if I needed any help. Years earlier while toying with the notion of being emancipated, I had vowed I would never accept assistance from my parents. I did, however, allow my mom to read a couple of books that were on my recommended reading lists for some classes so she could give me the highlights as I didn't enough time to read them. She obliged.

And finally, during that two-year period, just for giggles, and not to be considered a slacker, I committed to participating in an AIDS bike ride from Boston to New York. The team was called the Crown Hill Gang, and I trained with my boyfriend at the time and rode together for the event. I don't recall exactly how much money we raised, but I know it was over $5,000 as each person had to raise $2,500 in order to ride. We had one awesome good time! But damn, Connecticut sure had a lot of hills for being such a small state! I remember riding in the country outside the major cities and thought it was beautiful as we rode through quaint, historic towns; past barns that had been converted to artist's lofts, lush fields, and forests with ancient trees. But this ride was hard on those calf, thigh, and butt muscles!

Something's Happening Here

I was exhausted. I had carried a workload that was enough for three people. And now all of my graduations were scheduled on the same weekend! This was the culmination of two, totally intense years!

My family came to town. Some friends came to attend. I went to the bachelor's degree graduation on Friday night, and I received my commission into the Air Force as an officer on Saturday morning. I then attended the master's degree ceremony that afternoon.

My commissioning ceremony, a joint service ceremony with the Army and Navy, was impressive. These were typically plug-and-play-type events, but this one was different. The general was charged with reading the new lieutenants the oath of office was a dynamic and captivating speaker. He began his speech with the lyrics from the Buffalo Springfield song "For What It's Worth" and these lyrics stuck with me throughout the rest of my career. "There's something happening here...what it is ain't exactly clear..." The song was a Vietnam-era protest song but he reversed the meaning and message to have courage to defend a country that gave us the right to produce and sing that song. The something that was happening that day was a new generation of American military members stepping into the role of carrying the torch with courage.

The day I graduated from the master's program, I had a tear in my eye when I walked off the stage after receiving my degree. I was proud. As I walked down the short stairs at the end of the stage, gripping the thick, plastic folder with the certificate that signified my accomplishment as the first in my family to graduate from college, the first person to shake my hand was my advisor. She made her way down through the crowd. We hugged, we cried, we laughed, it was victorious as we celebrated that moment and I bid her farewell with thanks as I told her I could not have done it without her. She hugged me real close and whispered in my ear, "See, I told you no math."

I will never forget her for the gentle force that she was, a small petite woman who could help anyone dream larger than life. The kind of support and dedication this woman showed me just by believing in me and calling me to cheer me on from time to time was so special.

My father was there with his young, beautiful wife and their little boy, my younger brother. Surprisingly, my older brother and his girlfriend (not my favorite, as she was an addict that rained drama everywhere she went) also attended. My mother was there with her posse of friends from upstate New York. And, for some reason, I remember my gay uncle (one of my mom's brothers from her blended family) from Syracuse made it to my graduation. He said something completely inappropriate to my brother, along the lines of, "Not bad for a faggot!" as I walked up to receive a special academic award. Considering that I wasn't out to anyone in my family except my mother at that time, this was incredibly out of line! But then again so was he.

At the end of your ROTC commitment in college, a formal presentation event is held where graduates receive their first duty assignments. Like most graduations, these events are quite a production where family and friends are invited to the ceremony to recognize each new lieutenant for their achievements and to celebrate assignments as they are announced. My parents attended my high school graduation ceremony, but I never had this kind of event where my family could come watch me achieve such high honors. Up until this point they would only hear of my achievements after the fact.

It was an emotional day for me. I was fortunate enough to have my family live close enough to attend. But, as usual, my brother tried to grab the spotlight. He woke up hungover, and didn't want to go. My parents had to beg him, and then they had to keep an eye on him and his trashed girlfriend all day. I internalized the discomfort my parents must have been feeling as they were now divorced and my father was there with his second wife and young child. I was uneasy, not sure what my brother, parents, or other relatives might do. I preferred to have more control of my environment or better control at least, and members of my family made me feel like there was a loose cannon set adrift in my camp.

But my parents were pleasant, generous, and gracious. They presented me with a very classy graduation present meant for me to use in my new career. I can still remember the warm feelings of receiving the leather briefcase, which I knew was very expensive. They were so proud and happy for me.

The day was a whirlwind with all that I had to do. I was proud but exhausted. As I was getting dressed into my uniform for my ROTC graduation ceremony, wearing my bars for the first time on my blue uniform shirt, I felt I could talk to my inner child who promised himself he would become something and show them. I told that child that the promise was realized.

"You did it," I said to myself in the mirror. "You did it."

I sensed my family was proud that I was the first one in the family to graduate college, never mind having several degrees and being a commissioned officer!

I was astounded to see that most of my Crown Hill gang family also attended; Mary knew how to rally the troops in the neighborhood. And, not to brag, but I was very popular at school, so I had many friends in the audience. As the wing commander and prior service enlisted, everyone knew me. Plus, I was a respected commander. Even at just twenty-seven years old, after ten years in the military, I came to ROTC with a lot of experience.

My cadets looked on me as a leader and advisor and I took time to help them through issues, professional and personal, or answer active duty questions. I worked around my classes and work, family and social time, to make sure I supported my cadets to give them the best possible experience. I was rewarded in ways I could never have imagined at the ROTC graduation ceremony.

In an old brick building on the main campus at Worcester Polytechnic Institute, steeped with architecture and history, the active duty ROTC military personnel ceremoniously entered the ballroom and took their seats. Classmates and staff from my different colleges and many of my professors watched proudly as, for the last time, I—with rank of Wing Commander— led the procession of the ROTC cadets into the room.

As we marched up the center aisle in perfect formation, and synchronized steps, I no longer felt like a "less than" from Ballston Spa. I was large and in charge. Even I wanted to meet this impressive Mark D. Gibson to congratu- late him on his impressive accomplishments.

As I was sitting on stage, the sequence for the program in my hands, one of my fellow cadets, Andy, my Vice Wing Commander, took control of the ceremony. I wanted to yell at him and ask him what the hell he was doing. He motioned for me to keep my seat and said loud enough for everyone to hear, "I got this."

He had worked it out with the Cadre to surprise me. Then the lights went dim, the music started, and a photo montage about me played on a very large screen in front of the audience. It was a gift from my class, and definitely not the protocol for this ceremony. I was humbled and visibly moved as I held back the tears of joy and accomplishment. Andy came over and gave me a hug and sat next to me with his arm on my shoulder. The montage included photos the cadets took secretly and pictures they collected from friends and teachers on all three campuses and my life at Bose Corporation! I would never see them again after that day, but they each hold a special place in my heart and memories.

The music they selected as the soundtrack for the picture show was "Sweet Home Alabama." Honestly, I didn't understand why they were playing "Sweet Home Alabama." It's not like I played that music to anyone at school or had any special attachment to Lynyrd Skynyrd. Obviously, I was a little overex- cited and my brain did not connect the dots to put it together. My orders were announced, and I was heading to Maxwell Air Force base in Montgom- ery, Alabama.

"What?" I thought. "Nobody wants to go there!" I was still visibly moved by the ceremonial tribute presentation, but under my cheery façade, I was immediately depressed, angry, and sad about the whole Alabama deal. Of all of the cool assignments, I got Ala-freakin-bama? I had worked this hard for two years and my reward was a non-flying mission assignment to Alabama? I saluted smartly (I am a professional military man after all), and I followed orders. I went ahead and finished out the party. I packed my car and just went. I was heading to ALABAMA?!

As I left the parking lot, you could tell the difference in my age too because most of the new lieutenants were purchasing hot rods or motorcycles, anything fast and shiny red, but not me. I drove a forest green, Volvo 850 GLT, turbo-charged, twin engine. I loved that car. I set my course to Atlanta as a stopover for the weekend before heading south to Montgomery.

With time to think without interruption, and no alcohol to block my thoughts, I remember deciding on my drive that I wasn't going to be gay. I was going to be celibate. I was going to give everything up with regards to my sex life—just focus on being an officer and on advancing my career. For me it was only ten more years and I could retire. It would be a ten-year stint as an officer after having served a ten-year stint as an enlisted man with a two-year break between the two to finish all that schooling. (All that schooling that was sending me to Alabama!) I could embrace the real me, I resolved, after I left the military with all the benefits and pension that came with military retirement. They couldn't tell me who to be once I left service. It was something to look forward to.

When I reached Atlanta, I decided I was going to have one last hurrah as a gay man. Before I shut down everything inside me and became what I had to pretend to be, my last night of debauchery would include going out to gay bars. I checked into the Hyatt in midtown to be sure I was walking distance to ground zero of gay life in Atlanta. I was at Tenth and Peachtree and a short walk to Piedmont Park. It turned out that my adventure was as wild as I hoped it would be.

I had a really good time for my big gay finale. To add to the excitement, a new "friend" and I got stuck in the elevator between floors because of an electrical storm! A mechanic from the hotel was coming and would be able to slide the doors open. My "friend" and I took great advantage of the time we had in that elevator. The hotel manager called down the elevator shaft to see if I needed anything. "Yes," we shouted. "Send beer!" Such a classy end to my time in the Ivy League.

While out in Atlanta, I met a nice guy who was from Montgomery, Alabama, of all places—it's a small world! He gave me a phone number and said, "Hey, when you get to Montgomery, you have to look up so and so." I thought about it while driving the few hours to Montgomery, and decided I didn't have to be a gay guy calling a guy. I would go to meet new people and not be gay. Just a regular guy. But of course, I was playing tricks on my own mind. Pushing myself to be what society (or at least the military) was expecting of me. The same way that I changed who I was to please my family and the church.

One would think that after the whole debacle of my marriage and how hard staying closeted was on me that I would have learned to be more "me" in my life outside the job. No. I was only thinking about getting through the next few years and not having anything rock the boat. Nothing that someone could hold over me to ruin my career, like an ex-wife could do. I wanted safety and security, and I thought I was willing to give up my mind and heart and just become a robot going through the day. My work would carry me through. Yeah, right!

In Montgomery, I checked into the base, and began attending an aerospace basic class as part of my indoctrination to becoming an Air Force officer. After two years of school, and completing two degrees, I was heading back to school. Bitter, party of one, your table is ready! Returning to the classroom was NOT on the top of my list for activities. However, unlike most of my classmates, I was going to be assigned as permanent party in Montgomery for active duty. While attending classes, and while my classmates lived in barracks, I was provided with a temporary efficiency apartment, so I could get to know the area before I was fully living there.

Independence Days

I actually arrived at the base right before Fourth of July weekend. Everything was closed for the holiday or on administrative hold. I had a phone number in my duffel that I had received from the guy at that bar in Atlanta. Why not call the number? As usual, I was being circumspect and creating an entirely new persona for this undercover operation. I told the man that answered the phone that someone we mutually know gave me his phone number. The name of the person on the other end of the phone turned out to be Victor and, on the phone at least, he was a welcoming, polite, Southern gentleman. He invited me to a holiday pool party the next day. "Come on over," he offered warmly.

Being a patriot, why not go to a Fourth of July pool party? In my mind, I had my whole façade built. I would tell Victor that I was going to be transferred to the area with my job. I work for Bose, I would say. What I didn't realize was that when I was calling Victor, he had caller ID. In 1998, people were using caller ID all the time in business. I just hadn't even thought about it on someone's home phone.

I'd find out later that when I called for directions (this was before Google Maps and consumer GPS), the caller ID from my phone came up as Maxwell Air Force Base on Victor's phone. Busted. When he saw the call was from the base, he answered the phone and said, "Hang on a minute," and hollered out to someone there with him, "There's someone on the phone for you."

The mystery man got on the phone and I found out his name was Bryn. Bryn gave me directions on how to get to the house. I arrived at the party, opened the door hesitantly, as no one answered my knock or the doorbell, and made my way toward the noise I could hear at the back of the house. If it's a pool party, they must be out back at the pool, I surmised. When I opened the sliding glass door and looked at the pool, it was as though I was transformed to a set found in Hollywood. There was a sea of scantily clothed men. The music would typically be found in a club in New York or Chicago not at a barbecue for the Fourth of July in Montgomery, Alabama. The decorations were bright and colorful with pride flags everywhere and streamers in the wind hanging off the deck roof. Then I fixated on the pool. It was filled with DRAG QUEENS—all floating on giant inflatable, pink flamingos and other assorted inflatables!

These big-boned queens had the big hair to match. Lipstick. And attitude! I was suddenly mortified. "Oh my God," I thought. "What am I doing here?" From the exuberance of the crowd, the lack of inhibition, I was sure that a great number of drugs and lots of alcohol were being consumed. And here I was, a fresh new active duty military officer on the site of all this decadence! (I remember looking to see if anyone had a camera to ensure I was not in the frame.) I finally met Victor, by day—and Victoria, by night—when he came over to welcome me. She planted a big kiss on my cheek, which left bright red lip imprints on my pale skin. "Welcome to the South, Yankee boy," she squealed in a deep masculine kind of voice, loud enough for everyone to hear, as she smacked my ass. She also had huge Southern hair and offered me a drink or a bump (at the time I had no clue what that was, I just knew I didn't want it) and invited me to join the fun.

I glanced around the pool, taking in the colorful (and loud) surroundings, assessing the situation like any good officer would, when, across the deck, I caught the eye of a truly handsome man with short blonde hair, a chiseled chest, and a fine behind! He looked at me, from across the deck and we made eye contact, as if he could see my soul. I smiled. Without looking away, he rose out of his pool chair like a god being lifted from a throne and strutted toward my direction with a level of badass confidence that said, "Yes, that is right boys, look at me and my fineness." In the meantime, the queens all hooted and hollered about his fine ass and physique, deliciously poured into his swimsuit. As he approached he extended his hand, and introduced himself, "Hi, I'm Bryn, we spoke on the phone. Welcome." He was extremely confident and deliberate in his actions. I was mesmerized, not just by his smoking hotness, but by his entire demeanor.

Bryn and I had a normal first conversation. Bryn was forthright and explained that he and his partner were invited to the party but his partner had to work. But Bryn was in the military and was off for the holiday. I had come to the party with this big elaborate cover story with a fantasy job at Bose Corp, and, thanks to caller ID, my cover was blown right from beginning. But when I first met Bryn and Victoria upon arrival, I didn't yet know that they knew I was in the military. I had the military haircut and walked with a stiff and formal bearing. In retrospect, of course they had to know. They thought it was cute that I was trying to hide that fact. Holding a secret. Creating a façade. My life trying to repeat itself all over again in Montgomery. I hated it.

It seemed that no matter where I wound up, I had to submerge the true me, but yet again, people could actually see right through me. So why was I continuing to present myself in artificial ways?

I clung to Bryn for as long as I could. I learned he was from Texas. He was strikingly handsome, but not in a cowboy sorta way—in a GQ sorta way. He was very confident and not only smart, but very well read. He was very social, but not in an obnoxious way. I found myself fascinated by the fact that he was so open about being gay and being in the military.

When Bryn told me about his partner and how they met in Europe, his face lit up. He told me that his partner worked at the Montgomery mall, at the Bombay Co. store, "You should stop by and see him after you get your new place, he will help you gay it up." "That ain't gonna happen," I said to myself. Paranoid about drinking and driving, I just drank bottled water as we mingled and he introduced me to everyone he knew.

The party was winding down and I had to get back to the base—I mean Bose offices. Bryn gave me his AOL e-mail address. (I remember how exciting it was back then to dial-up and hear, "You've got mail," which I changed in my mind to "male.")

I was so enamored of Bryn. I wished for his level of confidence, for he truly was the Officer and Gentlemen I aspired to be.

I e-mailed Bryn after the party and asked to talk to him in person. I felt bad about the fact that I had basically lied to him about what I was doing in Montgomery. I wanted to know if I could meet him and his partner. He called me back and totally understood, he was very encouraging and kind. He was in a similar situation and he was determined not to hide. We discussed the Don't Ask, Don't Tell policy and started to forge a pact that unless they had pictures or videos, our private world would be our new religion. After all, in the Air Force and in the dirty, dirty South, religion wasn't illegal. We laughed.

Superspy that I am, I went out to the mall. I tried to see if I could get a glimpse of Bryn's partner. I stayed out in the mall, watching people wander around looking for inspiration, teenagers getting respite from restrained parental supervision, employees looking bored, until I finally saw who his partner was. I guess these days they'd call that stalking. Why did I feel the need to see this person? What connection was I feeling to Bryn that made this surreptitious behavior feel urgent to me? I just had to see for myself how he could do it and allow his sexuality to coexist with his military persona. I spotted his partner from afar. He was extremely handsome as well: tall, blonde with a very European chic presentation exuding confidence and a spirited personality as he pranced about the Bombay store. I'd come to learn that he was definitely comfortable in his own skin, had a snarky funny sense of humor, and knew music inside and out. By that fall we had all become fast friends and I had just about every piece of Bombay Co. furniture and framed pictures you could fit into a small house.

Bryn and his partner destroyed all my plans to retreat to the closet from which I came. We helped each other grasp hold of the highest levels of authenticity that we could possibly hold. We developed a tight circle of LGBT friends—high-ranking officers, to lieutenants like me, and enlisted members alike. Men, women—everyone was welcome in our circle of friends.

Our parties were elaborate and many. We were also open to other branches of service and became widely known as the gay military underground. Montgomery was the hot spot to visit, there was culture, restaurants, and the gay after-hours entertainment mafia was strong and well connected.

During the same time as the television series *Queer as Folk* (QAF) was released (we would host secret viewing parties), the Air Force was launching a new series of modules of self-paced professional development and history of the Air Force, entitled Quality Air Force (QAF). I was the marketing and communications one of the bunch and quickly drew parallels to establish codes while on official phones or e-mail systems. Both were QAF, but meant different things to different groups. I thought it was ingenious to call Bryn at work and leave word with his secretary that I needed to speak to him about a QAF matter. He would know to meet me and that my message had nothing to do with the quality of our Air Force, it was mostly to inform him that another "church member" or "family member" was on base. It felt so clandestine, but we made it work like oxygen, breathing life into our gay identities.

To this day, Bryn and I are best of friends. We have seen each other through tough times—during the winds of wars, he was in Iraq when I was in Afghanistan, to post-war time at home, and through battles with PTSD. I have grown very fond of his family and visiting their ranch in Texas. His mom is a two-time cancer survivor who inspires me to live bolder, louder, and stronger.

Senior Airman Mark David Gibson, 1987

Cadet Wing Commander Mark David Gibson, 1998

Riding for a good cause

AIDS Ride 3 participants getting ready

By Kathleen A. Shaw
Telegram & Gazette Staff

WORCESTER — Mark Gibson and Michael Butts of Worcester have very good reasons for joining the New York AIDS Ride 3 on Sept. 12.

Gibson's good friend has lived with HIV and AIDS for 12 years, and Butts has lost two of his closest friends to AIDS.

Gibson and Butts were among those who gathered last night at the Elks Club, 233 Mill St., to pass out signup sheets for the bicycle ride. Those participating in the ride will solicit pledges. "We have to raise $1,500 apiece in order to ride," Gibson said.

The local riders have been training for two weeks. "We have gone up Mount Wachusett, and on mountain bikes no less," Gibson said.

More than 3,000 bicyclists are expected to make the three-day, 275-mile journey from Boston to New York from Sept. 12 to 14. Last year's event brought in more than $6 million, and they expect to raise even more this year, according to the ride sponsors.

The proceeds will benefit HIV and AIDS-related services at Boston's

CHRISTINE PETERSON

From left, Michael Butts and Mark Gibson speak with Steve Davis of Boston. The three were working yesterday at a fund-raiser for AIDS Ride 3.

Fenway Community Health Center, the New York Lesbian & Gay Community Service Center and Community Health Project.

Last night's event brought out a number of supporters, with singer Roy Michaels of Boylston providing the entertainment.

Boston to New York AIDS Ride, 1997

1st Lt. Mark David Gibson, Langley Air Force Base, Virginia, circa 2001

The Living Years

I Try

One thing about military life that can be as equally appealing as it can be disheartening is the fact that we move around a lot. When I was enlisted, I was excited about my career choice's forced changes in scenery and increased challenges and responsibilities. But as the years passed, and I became an officer, it became very difficult to uproot my life, leaving behind friendships and support systems. And leaving Montgomery was no different.

The lower grade officers, of which I was one, were called Company Grade Officers (CGO). We had an unofficial volunteer professional development organization on the base. It was strongly encouraged that all lieutenants and captains become members and actively participate. The group did fun group activities and superiors looked favorably on participation. It was really a win-win situation to socialize outside of work and accomplish community involvement projects. I met Francis, a medical services officer, at these meetings and soon we were working on a committee together. A muscular, loud, bald Italian guy, he was short and stocky and dashingly handsome. I loved his confident demeanor.

He left shortly after for Langley Air Force Base in Virginia and would come back to Montgomery from time to time on official business. On one particular visit, he called me and said he was on his way over to my house to pick me up—he wanted me to take him to the "fun" places while he was in town. I was a nervous wreck having another military officer besides Bryn come to my house. I had little time to "straighten" the house but managed to shove anything "gay" into the hall closet before he arrived. Francis came twirling in, raved about the house and my Bombay Co. decor, and commented how great it would be for entertaining especially in the back of the house where the living room area was located. The living room in the back of the house opened up to very high eighteen-foot ceilings, with floor-to-ceiling windows. Since it was so far at the top of the highest window, in my haste, I forgot about a piece of stained glass artwork I got from Provincetown, Cape Cod.

"You straightened the house well but forgot one thing," he said without skipping a beat. I was about to pass out as he pointed up to the window where the pink triangle stained glass hung. Then in a commanding voice but with a sheepishly accepting grin he said, "Now take me out, bitch. I know you know where all the cool gay hangouts are here." This was coming from a married father of four.

It was in that moment I accepted the fact that I could somehow find a way to navigate the *Don't Ask, Don't Tell* policy while trying to maintain honest friendships. It was complicated, but Francis seemed to know how to be that perfect tour guide. And to this day, I value his unconditional friendship.

Macy Gray's, "I Try" was very popular at the time and seemed to play on every radio station every hour. Francis and I would crank it up and sing at the top of our lungs. This became my anthem.

I was in my early thirties and had been in Montgomery for a couple of years when I got the news that I was being summoned for another special duty assignment. This one was a by-name request and would require me to interview in person at Langley Air Force Base. I was excited at first because Francis was stationed there, but the more I learned about the job the more concerned I became. This was a protocol position for the four-star general. This job was reserved for the cream of the crop since the job entailed delivering a flawless image of the U.S. Air Force at all times. Protocol officers in the military are high speed, sharp as tacks, detail-orientated, and serious. No pressure! I was not all of those things—I liked to goof around and have fun at work. But being invited to interview is kind of like being "voluntold"—out of respect, you can't decline. I assumed they did a records review, which was admittedly impressive, but when I sat down for the interview I quickly informed the Deputy Chief of Protocol who was conducting the interview that there must be a mistake. I clearly was not the protocol officer type. We both laughed. As the interview was ending, I got up and thanked the interview committee for their time and the opportunity to interview. Out of respect, I wished them success in finding the perfect fit. She shook my hand and said, "We just did, you report in a month." My jaw hit the floor. "No, wait, what?" I tried to exclaim as she turned on her heel and walked away.

I met Francis later that afternoon to tell him what had happened. Protocol is a difficult demanding job, requiring very long hours and can be thankless—you're only as good as your last event. Francis laughed his ass off and was elated to have me joining him in Virginia. I affectionately responded by calling him a few choice words.

While it was very difficult to leave Bryn and his partner and our thriving underground gay network, I was comforted knowing Francis was waiting on the other end for me to arrive. As I drove out the main gate of Maxwell for the last time, I looked up in my rearview mirror and saw the base sign that greeted me a few years before...when I had dreaded pulling up. My Maxwell anthem, "I Try," began to play on the radio as I entered the highway. I opened my sunroof as tears fell down my face. My heart was breaking to leave Bryn just as it did so many years before when Tommy left.

When I arrived at Langley, Francis knew how difficult it was for me to leave my close-knit family, the gay underground, behind. He immediately took me under his wing and connected me to my new gay underground. He set me up with a realtor, found me a townhome, and helped me get settled.

It just wasn't the same. Nothing would ever be the same as those days back in Montgomery. And to think I went kicking and screaming to sweet home Alabama! But soon we would chart the course to create our own long-lasting memories!

I jumped right into the new protocol job. Protocol for a four-star general is no joke. It is fast paced and required long hours, so the time flew by. I really enjoyed getting to know the General and his family—true patriots and great Americans. The General's wife was smart, funny, and extremely supportive, but also demanded high standards in support of her husband and his role in showcasing America's Air Force. We got along very well, so well that I would wonder if she knew I was gay. But those thoughts would quickly pass, because honestly, I don't think either one of them cared one way or the other. (I just could not imagine thinking about one's religion, race, color of skin, or sexual orientation while demonstrating America's air power.) He would later be appointed the Chief of Staff of the Air Force (the highest position in the Air Force one could achieve), and I would attend his change of command event at Andrews Air Force Base in Maryland outside Washington D.C.—talk about protocol.

For the most part, my colleagues pushed each other to be better—better officers and better people. That deputy who interviewed and hired me went on to be promoted to the Chief of Protocol and became one of my favorite bosses. She taught me loyalty, dedication, and was the relentless epitome of excellence. It pains me that once again the wonderful, great Americans that I worked with and grew to love as my work family never experienced the true authentic Mark. I would later return many years later to Langley and surprise my old boss at her retirement ceremony. It was the stuff that dreams are made of as she hugged me and embraced me—the real me.

Gone to Carolina

After about four years, I left Langley and Francis and the wild experiences of a job I truly grew to love and enjoy. I found my true passion at Shaw Air Force Base in South Carolina.

A Public Affairs Officer for a Fighter Aircraft Wing was the coolest damn job in the Air Force. I found my niche. I loved the work, the people, the media engagement, and the mission. It was disheartening to not be open and honest about my personal love, but I managed to use the light of my purpose to chase away the darkness.

The Air Force had begun training us very early on to get into the mindset as a warfighter. We were assigned a training schedule and placed into a bucket-type system that included cycles of training, notification, and deployment. If you were in a training cycle you were not deployable, but if you were in the notification window, you could be deployed. If you weren't needed for deployment, you just continued the cycle until you were deployed. As the Public Affairs Officer stationed at Shaw Air Force Base in Sumter, South Carolina, I was deployable at any time as part of a warfighter package.

The first couple of cycles were no problem for me—training on base and then crickets, nothing would happen. But that changed during the third cycle when I was assigned to replace the Public Affairs Officer at Bagram Airfield, Afghanistan, north of Kabul. My mind went into full deployment mode. It was critical to get mentally prepared. A deployment is very stressful on the military member and their loved ones. And this deployment would be even more difficult because I could not admit to my comrades, my superior officers, or even the personnel office, that I had a loved one at home. In the eyes and records of the Air Force, I was a bachelor officer. Right, wrong, or indifferent, it was the reality of my life as a gay, closeted military officer.

When you're deployed into a war zone, you arrive with the knowledge that a world away there are loved ones living the life you left behind. And you hope that the life as you knew it is there when you return home. That thought shines like a lighthouse in the distance.

Terry and I lived on the second floor in the largest condo in the Tapps building on Main Street in Columbia, South Carolina. The condo building was a converted department store. We were in the bridal suite of sorts. The apartment was completely round.

Terry and I met when I was at Langley Air Force base and I lived in Yorktown, Virginia. He worked at a high-end hair salon in Virginia Beach. I found him charming, and handsome. He adored me and gave me a reason to enjoy coming home from my routine-oriented, stressful, military job. But there was always a mysterious third entity in the room that we did not talk about. My military life. It was off limits and I never talked about the details of my day.

Before I deployed, the parties we had were fantastic! Each party featured elements of decadence; proof of LIVING LIFE that embraced all our senses—chocolate fountains, champagne, live music. Any cause gave us a reason to have wild parties that would end up on the rooftop where everyone—straight, gay, bi—was welcome. Glamorous, loud, and memorable, like the parties of Hollywood's yesteryear.

Reality hit when I had to shuffle out of my building early one morning in full battle rattle gear and duffel bags for deployment. I didn't even tell the neighbors. I told Terry to let them know after I was gone. On my way out, I was spotted by a neighbor coming in from his morning run. He knew by the looks of the duffel bags that I was not going on a temporary or weekend "exercise." He was visibly shaken and when I went to shake his hand goodbye he went straight in for a long embracing hug. The embrace hit my emotions like a piece of ice on a back tooth.

We arrived on a sharp and rapid decent over the Hindu Kush in Afghanistan from 30,000 feet, a steep dive into a great valley basin where Bagram Airfield was located. Once landed, we deplaned, and I remember how difficult it was to breathe because of the elevation. The air was hot, heavy, and dusty.

Initially, my job was great. It was fast paced; the operations tempo "ops temp" was high. Being deployed there was always an opportunity to meet new people and get reacquainted with some I had not seen for a long time. The Air Force felt like a big family—so different from the family I grew up in. The Air Force's acceptance was predictable. You do a good job, "excellence in all you do," and you were recognized and loved (or at least rewarded).

Part of my job as a Public Affairs Officer was to highlight the positive works that air power was bringing to the fight, not just the thousands of pounds of munitions being dropped on the enemy. I tried to find good news stories and push them back to the members' units, or bases back home, and then to their hometowns by way of hometown news releases. Local papers loved to cover hometown hero stories. I was good at writing headlines for these feel-good stories, but sometimes my pithy, eye-catching headlines were not appreciated by the chain of command down range or back home.

For example, the unit I was currently deployed with, and aircraft that were hot on the ramp, were from Pope Air Force Base, North Carolina. The warfighting air package of A-10s would deploy with their staff support and maintenance teams. I would walk the flight line to capture random action photos of airmen working. Most of them knew me since I had a camera and was the only Public Affairs Officer. This one morning I was giving a "tour" of the flight line to a new chaplain that had just arrived. My camera, always on the ready, was by my side.

We wandered into a maintenance hangar, and I introduced myself and the new chaplain, who happened to be Catholic, to the group of airmen working on a jet engine. In a casual setting, airmen typically overlooked the chaplain's rank of captain or major and called them by their appropriate religious titles: Father, Rabbi, Pastor, Minister, etc.

As we made our way through the maintenance hangar to the engine shop, a young airman, covered in grease, came over while cleaning his hands on the rag hanging from his hip pocket, to shake our hands. Without skipping a beat, the chaplain (who we called "Father,") knelt down to bow and say hello. I immediately snapped pictures. We all laughed as the chaplain rose to his feet and stood tall, and we went about the rest of our tour. The new chaplain was pleasant to be around. He was extremely supportive, jovial, and fun.

Later, with the tour completed, I wrote a story about these incredible airmen working in extremely uncomfortable hot conditions, making sure the engines of the fighter aircraft were running in tip-top shape. Each one had pride in their work and knew that they were what kept America's air power in the air. I reviewed the photos and came upon the one where the chaplain had knelt to greet the airman. The airman's surname was Lord.

The photo accompanying the press release was priceless. The caption read: "Father kneels to meet Pope's Lord." (The chaplain ("Father") kneels to meet Pope Air Force Base's Airman Lord.) It went viral around the Air Force—in the way things went viral before social media! It was these good news stories, that from time to time, improved morale. I was honored to be the driving force as this work gave me opportunity to escape in my mind—to boost my own morale. They were both famous for a short spell. Everyone wanted to meet Airman Lord.

I was on the front lines and had the ability to push the information and photos quickly back to the States. I had only one deployment before in my career, so many years before, in support of Operation Desert Shield (prior to Desert Storm) to Riyadh, Saudi Arabia. But I was in more of a support function there. This time it was real, no kidding, in the heart of the war. I was a part of the pulse. The camp was continually under attack; alarms and warnings were a routine way of life.

During my seventy-two-hour transition period on to the base in my role as PA, the woman I was replacing briefly skimmed over the Fallen Comrade ceremonies while passing me the torch. She told me I "may," from time to time, be called upon to photograph the ceremonies. I attended only one photography class during Public Affairs training. The class mostly dealt with how to capture the photograph and what to do with it afterward. I'm no Pulitzer Prize-winning photographer, nor did I profess to be one!

These photos, she told me, would serve as the official photographs should the plane go down en route to the States. But that—that one brief comment—was the extent of my indoctrination and training. I was already horrified. What? Wait! Caskets? But she kept my training moving because our time was limited. I was not going to stand in the way of her boarding her plane home.

She quickly left on what was called the rotator. (A round robin of cargo planes that moved cargo and personnel into staging bases to catch commercial chartered flights back to the U.S.) I bid her farewell as she gave me a hug of support, "Good luck," she smiled. "You will be great!" was her vote of confidence. As she removed her hand from my arm and walked away, her departing shadow took with it the last of my support for this new role.

Some Gave All

As an ongoing reminder of how disheartening things could be in a war zone—yet another addition to morose occurrences—the midday alarm would sound signifying the next Fallen Comrade ceremony was about to begin. It was an unwritten requirement you would drop what you were doing to form up along "Disney" the main road of the camp named in honor of a fallen comrade.

Hundreds of soldiers, sailors, marines, and airmen would line up to pay last respects to the fallen. I was typically on the flight line waiting for the caskets to be loaded into the aircraft (a C-17 or C-130) on their way to Dover Air Force Base in Delaware.

A few weeks into my deployment, I got a call from the Air Force chaplain. We had become friends after that viral photo circulated around the world. We would share meals together and just talk. He was calling to ask if I would stop by his office. His tone was serious and I could tell this was not going to be a social call. I grabbed my hat and bottled water and left for his office.

There was something changing in the air at the base. Something raw. More exposed. My information was limited but I had heard the rumors that there had been an extensive battle overnight. In my mind, I assumed we kicked some serious Taliban ass. When I arrived at the makeshift chapel the mood was sullen. There were grief-stricken—some with tears in their eyes—soldiers, airmen, and marines lining the halls as I made my way to the chaplain. He pulled me aside to tell me what had happened in a low but stern, direct, command voice. "We took heavy casualties last night Mark," he reported.

The chaplain was in charge of the Fallen Comrade ceremony on the ramp of the airfield. He asked me to help. I needed to provide the photographic support. "Of course, no problem." He told me he would meet me at the Command briefing in an hour.

I departed through the same hallway, making eye contact with some of the soldiers. Their tear-filled eyes were sad, empty, and gray. It was almost like I could see through them rather than directly looking at them. I didn't know what to do to help alleviate their pain. My instinct was to hug them or put my arm around them, but I was an officer and that was just not going to happen. The only thing I could think of was to get to work, get busy, and get prepared. I think that many people did this in the war—a diversionary tactic to keep you from dealing with emotions or raw feelings.

At this point I had only witnessed a few relatively small Fallen Comrade ceremonies. They were powerful and moving ceremonies for even just one fallen comrade. I did not really think about the details at this time. I just went into checklist mode of what I needed to do to get ready for this service. I would await further instructions from the chaplain at the Command briefing.

I heard the commander was on the move over the "Brick" (a two-way radio on my desk), so I headed to the Hut where briefings took place. Inside, it was jam-packed and felt like 100 degrees as I made my way to my assigned position, gulping water. There was designated seating, based on the office or function, in the Hut. The commanders of each unit were typically around the table, and on the wall around the table were Public Affairs, JAG lawyers, and other support service offices. There were airmen sitting on the floor in the back of the room. This was highly irregular. The mood was solemn and quiet. Even when the commander came in and the room was called to attention (everyone stood swiftly at attention in front of their chairs), it was in a quiet, controlled manner.

The chaplain was a young guy, and I could tell he was nervous as he stepped forward to make the announcement. The commander took his seat and everyone followed his lead. First up was the Operations briefing. We learned that a U.S. Army Chinook helicopter had gone down the night before, and all souls were lost.

It felt like I was just kicked in the gut, I couldn't breathe. My eyes welled up. I just felt an enormous amount of sadness, grief, then pain and anger. The captain turned it over to the chaplain who explained ramp ceremony procedures and, like turning the page—with no time to wipe the tear from your eye—we were all focused on the task at hand.

I was having a quick conversation in my head, "No, no, no, you can't just burst out in tears in this briefing. Keep it together, Gibson." I also imagined how everyone else in the room was dealing with this. I gathered that some, the more seasoned or older, were accustomed to this and they were just numb. To me, it was horrible and painful.

Once the Operations briefing was over, the chaplain began to brief us on the ramp ceremony. This was different than the ones I had previously attended because of the vastness. I could tell by the formation of the aircraft on the ramp. In the past it was the C-130, smaller cargo aircraft. This time there would be a C-17, which was significantly larger than the C-130. I think it was at this point it occurred to me that the numbers were going to be high, but I still did not know exactly how many coffins were heading into this massive plane. But the number, I realized, was actually irrelevant to me as one lost soldier was one too many.

"Public Affairs will be on-site and Captain Gibson will provide the only official photographs," I suddenly jerked into attention. "Sir. Yes, sir." We received the time hack (a military term: everyone synchronized their watches to the current time) and then we were dismissed. Tasks assigned, responsibilities clear; everyone knew what needed to be done. The room stood swiftly standing at attention and waited for the commander to depart.

On his way out the door, the commander passed by me. "PA [Public Affairs]," he said. "Are you all set for the photography support?" I snapped to attention, stiff and erect and responded, "Yes, sir." He requested that I bring the photographs to his office prior to releasing them to HQ at the Pentagon. I again confirmed, "Yes, sir."

I had to take action. Back to my makeshift office, I checked my batteries. I was not letting my camera die on this assignment! I plugged in the battery charger and packed backups. I got water for staying hydrated, notepads, pens, and extra disks. What else should I bring? If I was busy and professional, I wouldn't think so much about this horrific event and what I was being asked to do for my country.

The caskets were too numerous to count. As they came around the corner from Disney, the procession just kept coming. It was overwhelming! Nothing you could ever do would prepare you for that sight. I was weary.

I knew intellectually that the identical polished metal boxes, draped with neatly tucked American flags, being loaded onto the tremendous aircraft like so many hope chests, contained dead and mutilated bodies. But I was disconnected. *Click/snap*…pictures taken to record the moment, serial numbers captured to correspond with caskets and names.

Years of leading a double life had split me into two people. One person with a face to the world that seemed cheerful and competent, unfazed; but the other persona was darker, depressed, hollow inside. I had fleeting thoughts that it should be me being loaded onto that plane—not the heroes in the pristine metal boxes—they presumably were not living a lie and did not deserve to die.

I knew that if I were not on duty, I would have gladly filled my consuming emptiness with alcohol. But no, general order number one in the theater was no alcohol allowed. There is no anesthesia; one must be sharp and ready to act. So, *click/snap, click/snap, click/snap*—I captured the endless scores of pictures for posterity and for the loved ones waiting around the world for their beloved to arrive. The photos were secured and protected in a locked cabinet, for use in the unlikely event that the aircraft went down with the precious cargo.

Once the photos were shot and the caskets were ready to be loaded, I remember hearing the command sergeants bellow out the command A T T E N T I O N which rippled across the flight line ramp. The band played "Taps," and one by one, the caskets were loaded and placed in position in the back of the C-17 with precision. I was already in position in back of the plane and continued to capture the footage, taking dozens of pictures. The caskets were lined up, end to end, secured in place. Rows of caskets. Rows of flags.

At this ceremony I counted seventeen caskets—the single-day, highest casualty count for the war up until that point.

As I climbed into the back of the cargo hold of the plane, the smell of death in the air, I felt like I was having an out-of-body experience. I could see my feet moving but I wasn't aware of how.

After all the caskets were loaded, the members of the unit that took the devastating loss were invited to line up and enter the aircraft from the rear. They had a private ceremony with the chaplain and departed through the front of the aircraft, single file, passing the caskets like a procession in a funeral home, all taking place on the back of an immense cargo aircraft.

Young, fresh faces lined with ribbons of tears, lips quivering with both sorrow and fear, stood at attention for the dead. "The lines of demarcation blur between the living and the dead, for we are aware that we may be next," I heard one of the marine colonels say, as I continued my photography assignment.

And so, part of our spirits departed with each casket. Those left to face the enemy wore looks of despair too old for their newly shaven and eager faces. Hope abandoned us; death surrounded us. Only the age-old rituals and ceremonies maintained any semblance of cohesiveness for us, binding us together in the surreal setting. We kept time while the tides of war slowly engulfed us.

That night I disappeared to the latrine to take a shower. I needed to be alone. I bit down on a washcloth to sob quietly as tears streamed down my face, hidden from the other soldiers under the cover of water. I wanted to retch.

I could not bear to stand on Disney and salute another flag-draped box or photograph another brother or sister going home; fighting in a country to allow the people of Afghanistan more rights than I, as a gay military man, would realize in my own country. My head was swirling out of control, but I didn't even recognize it because of the under-armor I was developing. I was accustomed to living a dual life under layers upon layers of denial, guilt, and shame.

Back in the office I spent hours adjusting the photos to ensure they were perfect before release—color correcting, stabilizing, centering—a form of perfection paralysis had set in. It was not unusual to work until three or four in the morning after an emotionally draining event like this. Seconds turned to minutes, minutes to hours, hours to days; they all ran together. In the morning, after the commander reviewed them, he looked up and said, "Good job," and asked if I was doing okay. "Yes, sir," I replied. I left and the photos were packed up and shipped off for safekeeping.

In truth, this was the beginning of my battle with PTSD. I just had no idea at the time.

Hope Delivered

One day we were encouraged to join an operation to deliver toys, supplies, and food to a nearby town. It was called Operation Pen. The children of Afghanistan absolutely loved mechanical BIC pens that clicked. They would gather in the streets and make the motion as though their thumbs were pressing and clicking the metal tops of pens. The first time I saw this I thought they were motioning to detonate a weapon or bomb. The security patrol sergeant laughed as he informed me it was for BIC pens. (I felt like an idiot; I didn't know.)

We assembled at the base of the tower in the center of the camp to learn our assignments on the mission: navigator, gunner, or driver. Everyone had a role on a convoy mission.

The sergeants loaded the back of the trucks and the Security Forces lieutenant told us the key to success of this mission was to stay alert, drop, and run. He was not worried about the enemy shooting or bombing us; he was more worried about a mob overtaking us, because we were going to hand out supplies, clothes, food, and toys. We needed to do it in an orderly and quick fashion.

As the ranking officer on this mission, the lieutenant asked me if I had anything to add. I *was* a Public Affairs Officer; I *always* had something to say! I informed the small detail of airmen and soldiers, "Remember to be respectful and mindful that life is hard here and there is little hope." (The very word "hope" I was certain was, or should be, consistent in any religious writings, whether it's in the Bible, the Quran, Hindu or Buddhist teachings.) I continued, "Be respectful and mindful that yesterday sucked here for them and there is little hope for today, and tomorrow proves to be the same. These small care packages of supplies, clothes, and toys will be, to some, the highlight of their year; like the best birthday or Christmas morning one could imagine. Don't raise your voices or make sudden movements. Keep your weapons on safety in the inner circles where kids are present. In the outer circle of security, remain vigilant. Let's roll."

About an hour away from base camp we arrived in the small village in a blaze of dust, as the convoy was moving very fast. A cloud of dust and dirt passed over us; the lieutenant and I emerged from the vehicle with our translators to officially greet the mullah. Typically, the mullah is the oldest gentleman in the village who provides wisdom and spiritual leadership to the village. I learned that the mullah was also how the village got their current events, news, and information.

We instructed him that we would place the donated supplies in a loading area on the edge of the village as we had concerns of a mob forming. He indicated he understood, and assured us it would not happen. We asked him to fairly disseminate the supplies. He agreed and grabbed my hands and pulled them close to his chest and heart with thanks. His skin was liked sun-aged leather with wrinkles; his eyes were tired and yet still illuminated with watery gratitude and sincerity. I was deeply touched. The security detail got a little tense when the old man touched me, but I told them it was okay.

There were no women in the village streets to be seen. I did notice a few of them hiding and peeking from around the side of their mud hut buildings.

I asked my translator to ask the mullah if it would be okay if our troops met some of the children to give them toys. Again, concerned about a mob situation, and the fact that we had loaded weapons, I needed him to rally some adults in the village to help facilitate an orderly receiving line. An adult would accompany a child in the center of a field, then a soldier would walk toward the two of them and hand the child a toy—one by one and in an orderly fashion.

The air was tense, the Americans were eager to please and bring gifts, while the security detail wanted nothing to do with it and verbally protested as remaining in this village was a significant security risk.

The kids were typically shy, but a couple in particular took a liking to me. I think they felt comfortable because I was with the mullah. One kid hugged my left leg for a long time and would not let go. This made me nervous as my 9-millimeter pistol was strapped to my thigh on the right side. It didn't exactly thrill my security detail either!

The toy distribution was an opportunity to escape the monotonous day-to-day and the depressing Fallen Comrade ceremonies, and I cherished the moment. As I looked into the eyes of the children and the adults involved, I smiled as I recollected my own excitement at holiday times as a child. I wanted to know EVERYTHING. I was insatiably curious. I loved candy and toys and traditions. I could sense what these children might be feeling as we brought cheer and fun into their difficult lives. The whole toy exchange was emotionally moving for not only me, but for all the men and women on the detail this particular day.

For a minute the sharp fangs of the enemy and the war were retracted, but only for a moment. I heard a message on the radio and looked to the security detail who made a circular motion with his finger in the air, ("round it up"), and it seemed that just as fast as we breezed into the village, we were whisked away.

There were reports of unidentified vehicles moving at a fast pace from the south. Hearts racing and battle rattle clanging, we were off like a dart on our way heading back to base camp. I talked to Omar (the interpreter) on the journey home and asked him if we had placed the village in jeopardy because we favored them and provided supplies etc. He sadly indicated that this was true. But it was up to the mullah to make the ultimate decision.

The enemy wanted nothing more than to keep the people of Afghanistan down and out, just barely surviving and getting by with no hope.

We visited that village a few more times before I left Afghanistan. The mullah and I talked about assistance in helping him and the villagers drill a deeper water well. He had shown me during the initial visit where the well had run dry. He needed tools to drill into the lower aquifer. He was not letting me leave without a commitment to help him and his village. I agreed and again he grabbed my hands and placed them on his chest, as he began to weep. Even my security detail was moved by this sight of appreciation and compassion.

I would later write up this story and send it to major news outlets around the world with stunning photos and images to capture the emotions of the moment. I would continue to champion these efforts and tell anyone that would listen about the hearts and minds that wanted peace not war.

My commander, the General, loved the PR program and was impressed with my passion to get the positive experiences out to American communities. Older, wiser, and more astute than I, he knew the reality of the day would lead to headlines about war, death, and dying as civilizations looked on—if it bleeds, it leads. I jumped to an immediate counterpoint, upon which he totally agreed with me. "But, sir, the enemy wins when we don't counterpunch with all the good the coalition is doing in country." We would save this debate for another time as his calendar was jam-packed.

Disheartened, I reached back into my memory banks for an idea I dreamed up so long ago, when I wrote a letter to Ted Turner proposing a brand-new concept in news reporting: the Good News Network (GNN). This would definitely be a platform for stories like the one I just told. A patronizing, "Yes, Captain Gibson," and the General would dismiss me, as I was ushered out of his office with a gentle smile of encouragement. I smirked at myself as well, because I knew the General's reality was getting jets launched that were loaded with precision-guided missiles and smart bombs. So back to work I went.

Hero's Welcome

Funny how the time goes by quickly when you are working twelve to fourteen hours a day, six days a week. Quickly my four-month deployment was coming to a close. Sadly, the doors of my memory were also slamming shut. Everything I had heard, seen, and experienced there at the foothills of the Hindu Kush were seared into my memory. But, like everyone, I was excited to be going home.

The trek home was long, and while the decompression starts right away for most, it was not the case for me. I was always on guard for something or another—not paranoid, it was just the reality of everything you'd do in one day to keep up a façade.

We flew through Europe and had a layover in Ireland. The bars in the airport concourse were filled with American soldiers. The hospitable Irish would not accept or allow any of us to pay for a beer. I followed the merrymaking with a couple of "no go" pills (Ambien) and boarded the next charter aircraft to cross the pond and try to get some sleep. First stop: Hartsfield International Airport, Atlanta, Georgia.

Hartsfield had this down to a science; an airport official greeted the plane and escorted us to a separate customs area in the belly of the airport. Afterward, in a group in two single-file lines we walked through the airport to our next processing point. Along the way, people stopped and lined the hallways, and with thunderous applause, they clapped, cheered and high-fived as we passed by. America, home of the free because of the brave—these spectators were genuinely proud of us, and I suspect did not care about one's religion, skin color, or sexuality. It was definitely a hero's welcome home. One by one we would bid each other farewell as we scattered to our different gates to take us to our home units all over the U.S.

From there, still high and proud from the hero's welcome, I hopped on a short connector flight up to Columbia, South Carolina. For most military members, arriving home in the U.S. resulted in extreme excitement and pure joy that would often produce tears. Not for me. I never got to experience a hero's welcome by having a loved one meet me coming home.

Although I did have a few boyfriends who would have been bold enough, it was absolutely out of the question in my mind, especially in uniform. If they would attempt to surprise me like that, I would have walked right on by as if I didn't know them. In retrospect, I was so shortsighted. Other men greeted men, and I did not immediately jump to them being homosexuals. Oh well, it was the life and walls I built. My lovers never got the flight information. They seldom even got the exact day that I would return. *Don't ask, don't tell.*

A House Is Not a Home

I t took a while to settle back into a fast-paced work routine and everyday life. I walked around almost like an extraterrestrial at first. I felt odd and out of place. Everything had continued to move forward while I was away.

I was fortunate that I had a great job to come home to. I loved being the Public Affairs Officer for Shaw Air Force Base, even if it was in Sumter, South Carolina, which was not exactly a thriving metropolis. Don't get me wrong; the people were amazing and wonderful: top-notch, patriotic, God-fearing Americans who loved me back only because of the uniform. I assumed that some would just as soon burn me at the stake in the middle of town if they only knew.

The community around the Air Force base was one of the most patriotic places I have been, even more than Washington D.C. I was very proud to wear the uniform and represent America's Air Force, until the long drive home each day to Columbia, where I would shed my military uniform and mindset and segue into comfy clothes and gay man mode. I seldom lived in the community where I was stationed.

In Columbia my one-year lease was coming due on the luxury loft apartment down on Main, which was overpriced for my budget anyway. It was far more practical to chart a course to purchase a house. Interest rates were low and my Veteran's Administration (VA) eligibility would get us a mortgage half the price of the rent.

I devised a plan to purchase a house, but no amount of guilt was going to allow me to get financially involved on paper with a person that didn't actually exist according to my military personnel file. I was single, lived alone, no partners. I was all about the Don't Ask, Don't Tell policy but did not want to flaunt anything either. Therefore, my boyfriend at the time, Terry, who worried about me while I was at the war, and maintained the home front, was never going to be an equal, nor realize his true relationship potential with me. It was sad actually because I knew just like the ones before him, it was never going to work. I was too guarded and no one was getting in or that close to me, not even members of my family. With the oath I had taken so many years before came a price. That price was living a life without authenticity.

Somehow, I would keep the plates spinning. Terry and I found a quaint, low-country cottage house on a double lot not far from downtown Columbia. Adorable, charming, in the style of a Charleston cottage from the front, it looked small. But when you entered the sunny home, you found three floors and tons of space. The home dropped down a hill in the back, making the inside of the cottage actually quite large. I loved it and it was quite affordable. My precious dog Gena ran around and around enjoying all the open space in the house. She LOVED the large backyard!

The only thing Terry brought to the table was excitement about the house. He never had any money. I once again would overcompensate and let my guilt and fear of being public about our relationship cloud my judgment; providing all the resources to support my partner without getting much back.

Terry and I settled into a soothing routine in our adorable cottage with my Gena, the best dog in the world. We kept to ourselves and seldom interacted with the neighbors, which was not like me at all. I was an officer, gentleman, and past neighbors had always shown their appreciation for having someone so helpful and friendly next door.

I did, however, manage to befriend an elderly neighbor directly behind my house. I could see his kitchen from my back deck where I let Gena out every day. Bill was the second elderly military man (both oddly named Bill)

I had lived next to during my career that I took a liking to. He was very frail and didn't drive, so I would shop for him at the commissary and bring him groceries from the base.

We had a system that worked out just like the system with the first military Bill I lived next to, back in Cheyenne. I would have them put up a particular shade for me in the house, so I would know they were okay. I would promptly knock on their door if the shade was not up when it was supposed to be. Sadly, in both cases, my heart broke to find them as a result of the shade down. Both of these strong men died alone in their homes. They would try to talk about dating the lovely ladies and reminisce about their youth. I would deflect or change the subject and listen to their war stories for hours on end. I had a bond with them and think they both actually "knew" the deal.

Nothing to Bragg About

The Air Force Deployment rotation plan that was sold to us by our commanders was not perfect, but it was the best system that they could come up with regarding moving a large amount of personnel in a short amount of time. Basically, you were assigned to a "deployment bucket." In theory, the bucket worked like this: When your number came up, you deployed for three or four months; upon return you would go inactive for rest and recovery, and then you would be placed into a cycle for the next possibility of re-deployment after a twelve-month period. In between, you were supposed to be training and be prepared and ready if needed.

I got notified from HQ that they had an out-of-cycle deployment requirement for Public Affairs Officers that needed to be filled. It was between me and another woman. I didn't sweat it, as I had just returned only six months before and she did not have a single deployment under her belt. I kind of forgot about it, almost as if I was in denial, until I got the call from the Pentagon letting me know I was selected. "WTF? How can that be?" I fumed. It turned out that the woman was, a little too conveniently, pregnant and not deployable. I had no choice at this point but to salute smartly with eighteen years of service. "Just my luck" I thought, "I was going to be one of those bank robbers who got caught or killed during the last hold up." There was nothing I could do about it but get ready—emotionally, personally, and professionally.

Emotionally just meant financially supporting Terry and ensuring the house was a castle for my dog. I also worried about my mother. She was living alone in upstate New York, but I felt reassured knowing that she had a nice support circle of friends.

My mother came to South Carolina to bid me farewell as I was settling last-minute details for this second Afghanistan deployment. I insisted that Mom address logistical things, like a last will, with me. The Air Force requires that every airman have a last will and testament. This time, perhaps because I had seen the theater in my last deployment and saw how many caskets were sent home, I wanted my mother to have copies of all my documents and to understand my wishes and intentions.

My intention was to provide support for Terry while I was alive, but Mom would get all of my assets, sell the house, and take the dog. I suspected she would probably put Terry out on his ear if I should die. They weren't close, mainly because she didn't like that I supported him. I made sure she had the life insurance details and burial wishes for cremation. I did not want to be buried in soil of a country that I would have died for but did not allow me to live authentically.

Mom was good under pressure, and supportive in her way, until the day she was leaving and could not hold back her tears any longer. Sobbing, yelling at me, telling me she did not want me to go back as we stared at my military issued deployment duffel bags packed and ready at the door. I just gave her an empty, reassuring hug.

This deployment was in support of the Army and would be eight months—twice as long as my previous four-month stint. I knew things were like a house of cards between me and Terry; through no fault of his own. Terry, along with family and friends were all pushed aside or hidden in recessed alcoves of my closeted emotions, heart and mind. Nothing would fit except cold numbness of duty and service. I continued to stuff my feelings into any open bottle of vodka or can of beer I could find. Happy, energetic on the outside; dark and dying like slow-moving lava on the inside. The cancer of lies and hate ate at my soul.

The next deployment required eight-weeks of training in Fort Bragg, North Carolina, and proved to be an eye opener as the Army trained very differently than the Air Force. The now-faded memories of my first visit here were the exact opposite from what I was experiencing—and this caused a weird double take in the mirror of my mind. Weapons training, convoy maneuver training, psychological operations, information operations—the list went on and on. The Air Force was always considered the most corporate of all services, but the Army training was dormitory living again in pre-WWII barracks, with horrible open bays. Luckily for me, I had driven from South Carolina, so I had a car that hid food and vodka, because the chow hall had powdered eggs and freeze-dried meat and other non-edibles!

I would try to sneak off base as much as possible and drive home to see Terry. I do believe he loved me. At a minimum, he loved my vitality, tenacity, and bright outlook on life, oh and my checkbook.

Terry lacked motivation, capacity, and enthusiasm—all attributes for which I would overcompensate for—to make up the slack. Nonetheless, I could sense he was pulling away from me, perhaps his way of dealing with the fact that I might not return home. It was horrible. Perhaps it was his reaction to me shutting down my emotions as I readied for duty and another deployment.

I would drive late Sunday night to make it back to base camp, and sneak back into my bunk before Monday morning roll call. My sadness and tears at home with Gena turned to stone and anger on base. I had to put my head in the game called Army and get ready for this deployment.

My trips home would become less frequent as I could not bear the sadness in Terry's eyes. It was always safe with using the "restricted to base" excuse. I did return home one final time to leave my car as my Army compatriots and I were headed across the pond. Terry was cold and lacked any emotion; everything was routine; even the food was bland. I took baby girl Gena for many, many long walks, talking to her the entire time. Such was my charming home in Columbia, South Carolina—a beacon calling to me, to ensure I wanted to come home instead of climbing into one of the flag-draped coffins I once photographed.

We arrived in-country, this time to the Army side of Bagram Airfield in Afghanistan. Everything looked just the same, I laughed to myself. Nope, I didn't leave anything here.

I remember getting off the cargo plane and taking my camera out as the Hindu Kush was radiantly snow-capped, I was harshly reminded—no cameras allowed. I knew that, but in my old role, I was one of only a few that had permission to take photos on the flight line. A glimmer of the shiny flagged-draped caskets flew through my mind; I wondered which one would be mine.

Again, it did not take long to get into a routine when the duty day was fourteen to sixteen hours long and the other hours were for eating, sleeping, laundry, or sometimes working later. I set up a routine on how to reach my family back home. Terry was seldom "available" for the scheduled morale phone calls. There wasn't much we would be able to talk about on an unsecure line anyway, so I would patch my morale calls into Mom or other friends and family.

I was able to do the "Mark Show" for Mom. I think she felt relief to hear the laughter and distractions I would make to shield her away from the reality of death that lingered with each mission. But creating an alternate reality, a cheery variation of Mark, was exhausting. I couldn't bear to think of my mother suffering like I was—not sleeping, wrestling with demons, thinking you're going crazy. She needed to feel hope and I needed her to be happy. Pretending to be fine for her made it easier to get through my day too.

I craved alcohol to quiet the marching band stomping through my brain during quiet hours. Instead, I spent my spare time helping Terry develop his dreams of owning his own hair salon and launching a product line. I worked on his business plan, product line, and website. It was an escape for me.

Having gone through the Disney line-up and tribute during the first deployment, I found it was no less unsettling this time around. Someone at home was going to be visited by a soldier in uniform with a monotone delivery of a prewritten statement and the presentation of a triangular-folded American flag. Someone at home was going to be making burial arrangements for their loved one. Tears would be shed. I could not shed any more tears. I wavered between fearing and wanting to be back with my family, reintegrating myself again into "normal" life and wanting to be in one of the departing boxes with all the inauthentic baggage I carried into the theater with me.

Devastation and Civility

There were days when I thought I might find the local culture of Afghanistan interesting if I were there under normal circumstances. As the Information Operations Officer of the Provincial Reconstruction Team (PRT), I had developed a respectful rapport with three of the local leaders, two were sitting governors. One was a senior statesman appointed by President Karzai. They were good men, leading a strong but weary people through a trying time in a difficult place.

The PRT had an incredible mission, charged with the daily responsibility of providing support and services for the people of Afghanistan who were stuck between the terrorists and the peacekeeping troops. I was the public relations element of the unit, charged with developing cohesive working relationships to ensure message continuity with the provincial government, the Afghanistan President's office, and the coalition forces. We brought electricity and roads, running water, and other amenities that Western cultures take for granted, but were not easy to find in the middle of mountains and rough terrain and desert sands. The hope was to encourage the population of Afghanistan to help us in our fight, so they could have their land back and live in peace.

The terror groups preyed on naïve and poverty-stricken children, converting them into mini-warriors and martyrs. America recruited young, idealistic people to join in the fight for democratic and "civilized" living—to protect the American way. Both cultures thrust war and conflict on impressionable minds way too early. I joined at seventeen years old and it wasn't until I went through my first Afghanistan deployment and saw the caskets that I realized what I had committed to do. I always knew in the back of my mind, but until that upfront and personal experience, it wasn't made real.

The people coming to relieve the active duty troops were largely made up of young reserve troops comprised of department store managers, farmers, and bankers from all over the Midwest. These young people saw war on television, movies, and video games. To some they had the mentality to kill kill kill and couldn't wait to use their weapons—a dangerous and deadly motivation to have when facing off with real weapons and an evil, remorseless, soulless, enemy. I don't think anyone is ever truly ready for war. When reality hits and the people standing beside you are blown to bits, the excitement and adventure wears off quickly. Survival instincts kick in.

Daily missions would require us to be outside the confines of the base. We arrived in the local villages of Afghanistan, where eager, young, American National Guardsmen quickly provided protection by surrounding me with loaded weapons, securing our perimeter, and positioning vehicles for quick departure. Always on alert; ready to defend.

Upon our arrival, it did not take long for the local children to amass with their sun-worn skin, large dark eyes, and larger white smiles as they flocked around us, positioning their fingers in the air to click imaginary pens. As I learned during my previous deployment, the kids loved American-made pens, or any other gift for that matter.

The first time a soldier arrived, one might have thought it quaint that the children were enamored by something as simple and abundant at home as pens. However, we were all too aware that these clicking pens could be used to signal a distant shooter or to detonate any one of the children that might be strapped with explosives. Our enemy on the ground had taken note of our love of children and watched as we distributed pens to anxiously extended hands and happy smiles. They used this against us—converted pens into a signal for bombs, a detonation device, just as I had suspected during my first deployment. Like lizards adapt to the color of the ground below them, the Taliban adapted to Western habits and changed the way they terrorized and attacked to blend right in.

This enemy was just as ruthless as conquerors, oppressive rulers, and dictators who came before in history. Women and children were not sacred. This Taliban enemy studied Western culture and knew that Westernized cultures, like the Americans and Europeans, buckle to women and children. It is in the fabric of the Western psyche. Much like Hitler and the Third Reich, this enemy had little regard for women and children. How does one compete with that?

I remember chastising the new guys for trying to offer soccer balls to kids in a country littered with land mines! I had to point out that any innocent detour into the surrounding land to retrieve a wayward ball might lead to being maimed or killed. How many countless goats exploded into a mist of fur and blood and bone in advance of our party? Sacrifice without remorse.

War-Torn Home

After a couple months into the deployment the weather was turning colder. One evening, as I was sitting in my hut wearing makeshift mittens cut from clean socks and flipping through e-mails, I felt a jolt of harsh pain. It was immediately apparent that this one particular e-mail had not been intended for my eyes. It was from Terry, my lover back home, asking the recipient about his HIV status. "I don't normally do this bare, but not to worry, right? We ARE both negative?"

The e-mail right after that was my electronic monthly bank statement. I could see my balance in the preview pane. It was very low. As I read on, I realized my bank accounts were being siphoned off while "Mark's a million miles away." Frantically trying to open my bank accounts on the ever-so-slow internet there, I read the bank statements as my eyes scanned the pages, my breath coming in shorter and shorter gasps. All the pent-up emotion now flooded me with rage. I had to get home, and fast. I was desperate! My mind was racing back and forth like a trapped rat in a maze, getting more and more anxious to get out.

The harshest part was that I had a life I couldn't explain or share with anyone. As far as the military was concerned, I wasn't married. For all intents and purposes, I was a single, heterosexual, white male, and these secret problems were not real and thus could not be used to explain why I HAD to get home. I cursed the document I signed so many years before in exchange for this uniform; for the privilege of defending Afghanistan, while I was deceiving my own country.

My mind shifted into overdrive to quickly draft a plan to persuade my superiors into letting me go back home to the States immediately. I called in a favor. The General didn't ask, and I didn't tell. It was a family matter, an emergency. I was able to combine this "emergency" with an official military matter. Right around the same time we had received an official by-name request for me to return to Fort Bragg, North Carolina, to provide training for soldiers getting ready to deploy. This coupled with my status as a good officer and clout from my overachieving energy was the only thing that got me on board the next rotator heading to the States.

I learned there was a cargo plane leaving within a few hours. I hastily threw some things in a duffel bag, grabbed my weapon, and began yet another bumpy, long journey home to the U.S. of A.

I had not slept in a few days—with scenarios of what I'd find at home playing like movies over and over in my mind. We had a layover in Kuwait for a few days and it felt like I was actually losing my mind. Suddenly, I could not discern the voices in my head and those around me as they all seemed the same and real.

By the time I reached the U.S., I was in shock, moving like a shadow, a faded representation of who I was, making it through all the hurdles, until I landed, this time unceremoniously back in Atlanta, Georgia. I called ahead to Fort Bragg, North Carolina, and let them know I was delayed en route, so I could make an unofficial stop in South Carolina. "No problem, Captain, take your time, see you when you get here."

I ran to the rental car desk and jumped into a midsize car, which later would prove to be as fast as a stealth fighter, making my way to Columbia. I was on a mission.

I arrived in Columbia at breakneck speed. As I pulled up to my quaint, low-country cottage, I felt a sinking feeling. The cottage, like me, was a faded representation of what it had been. I was a ghost looking at ruins. Some windows were cracked and one was broken and cardboard-filled, shrubs were overgrown and unkempt, as was the unmanicured lawn. I brushed the dust away from the tiny pane of windows to the left side of the red front door and I could see Gena's tiny anxious face looking back at me. This alone calmed me. Knowing Gena was there, I could muster the courage to enter the house. But it was locked; the electric code on the lock had been changed. I peered through the window again and my eyes found trails of garbage and filth on the hardwood floors.

I remember dropping my bags and jumping off the porch. I walked the perimeter to the back of the house. Someone had broken the railing on the upstairs balcony, splitting the hot tub when they landed. And all while "Mark was a million miles away."

The house was locked up and I was freakishly peering in the windows. Like Jack Nicholson in *The Shining*, head peeking through the partially open wood door, where he sneers deliciously, "I'm baaaaack!" I thought angrily.

I jumped back in my land jet midsize stealth rental and drove to my boyfriend's salon. The secret to any stealth mission is an element of surprise. Opening the door to the salon, I was met with throbbing dance music and people sitting in chairs with foil and goop on their hair, under dryers, in front of mirrors, leafing through magazines mindlessly, and happily chatting or engaging in gossip with members of the flamboyant, less-than-honorable staff.

Terry was cutting someone's hair when he noticed my reflection behind him. I stood there in full uniform, my weapon at my side. Like in a movie, slowly the voices became hushed, one by one people ceasing movement; only the beat of the music filling the awkward silence.

"What are you doing here?" he asked, more curious than surprised. I never gave my partners the exact information of when I would return home, but they usually had some idea that I was coming home.

I think the nonchalance of his inquiry was the most shocking thing I experienced that day. Was he this stupid, this reckless, this arrogant? Or was he just unconcerned, a sociopath who had taken advantage of me?

In a deep, authoritative, and controlled voice, I commanded above the throbbing back beat of the music, "Give me the keys to MY house." My presence at the salon was completely unexpected, and it wasn't until Terry saw the red anger in my eyes and heard the cold command tone in my voice, that he realized this wasn't a "Surprise, honey. I'm home!" visit.

He nervously scribbled the new code on a piece of paper and disconnected the house key from the tight grip of his keychain. As he handed the key to me, I could see that he knew it was over. His self-indulgence had gone too far.

I left with my heart broken, but I couldn't feel a thing. I was running on pure adrenaline. On my way back home, I stopped at the neighborhood store to stock up on my "anesthesia" of vodka and beer. I was certain that the night would require much. My vision was black and white and dull and, while I assumed the flowers at the front of the market were of bright colors, I saw only gray shades; I bought a bouquet just the same. I arrived home and threw open the doors and swept my dog up off her feet as she welcomed me with boundless joy, as though I rescued her from a living hell.

I carried Gena around the house, as signs of Terry's sloth were everywhere. I kicked pizza boxes and empty bottles into scattered piles. It seemed like hours before I would let her down, but when I did, Gena was met with a clean placemat, fresh, bottled water, new fresh food with some tuna fish juice (a special treat she loved), and a bouquet of flowers next to her place setting. I wept and promised her I would never leave her alone again with anyone that would abuse her. I cried until there were no more tears.

Meanwhile, Mom in upstate New York was berserk after receiving many cryptic messages from me from the war zone, then Kuwait, then Atlanta, then home. I called her to give a status report—military brevity at best with no time for squishy, lovey, mushy talk. She heard distance and pain in my voice.

Rallying her troops, she rang the battle cry and jumped in the car with my brother and a longtime family friend. It was odd to me that my brother would join my mom on this mission. I can only imagine those phone calls as my mother (calm, cool, and collected) seldom rings the bell. But when she did, the backdraft from action could have blown you over. She knew how to work it.

The rescue squad drove all night to reach me in South Carolina. Broken but still talking, trying to feel close, but my body and spirit were still jumping into flag-draped boxes a million miles away.

Mom's gentle encouragement and countless hours on hands and knees to clean the filth eventually repaired the outward appearance of yet another home. Meanwhile, the dark corridors remained rampant with disappointment. Mom couldn't wash or sweep that away.

My older brother was wracked with grief and astonishment as he gazed off into space in disgust as the ice cubes would clink in his perfectly mixed vodka and cranberry concoction he would whirl with his index finger. He could not understand how anyone could do this to his younger brother. Never before did I feel as close to my brother as at that very moment. My brother gently, but with a firm grip, grabbed my shoulder and squeezed it; a sense of solidarity that we would get through this. His handyman skills could help my home, but they could do nothing against the rabid dogs at the gates of my soul. I was fighting battles and wars on so many different fronts; I was drained.

While family and friends were making my house presentable, I had gone on my boyfriend's computer to investigate just how much damage I had really sustained. To my horror, I discovered that he had used the basement of our home to make porn films, and some of the participants' ages were questionable at best. This was all I needed! The fear of him outing me and the inevitable, dishonorable discharge was always looming in the background like the Taliban hiding in the tree lines of the Hindu Kush. I ran over Terry's computer with my rental car, several times! Grinding my teeth I thought, "Take that, you son of a bitch."

I took Terry's prized collection of guitars and stashed them at a friend's place as collateral for all the damage he had done to my home. Terry loved his guitars more than himself, though he could not play a single note. I never did get paid back and the pawn shop was barely interested in the guitars. Figures.

My family helped me board up the house, I left Gena in the trusted care of a friend, and I returned to the war zone. Though I was just "home" for a while and saw family, I still felt like I had no home.

After a quick trip up to Fort Bragg I got into the rotation to start the long journey back to the war. This time feeling defeated and soulless, empty inside. Life for me was smothering the flame inside to just embers. I found myself staring off into the distance out the window of the airplane while most people either slept or watched movies or read. I was not much for conversation; it's a good thing the organs in the body operate automatically. I finally arrived and got right back to work the same day, just jumped back on the conveyor belt of the war and picked up where I left off. I got back to my bunk later that night and on top of everything I had to unpack and make up my living quarters again. When you depart for an extended period of time you pack everything up in foot lockers with your name and information just in case your personal belongings have to be sent home. I just grabbed my pillow and hit the rack.

Hope to Ashes

In Afghanistan, the Taliban is considered as much a part of the landscape as the land mines; unseen yet entrenched and of little consequence to the locals if left in peace. But we are in this dusty, dry land to help the innocent natives. American envoys came to villages to entice the local officials with a glimmer of hope. Sometimes it was the promise of water, electricity, or roads. On this day, we offered to build a school for the little youngsters who gleefully scampered around our troops' feet clicking their fingers for pens.

In return, we asked the town officials to give up or not support the "bad guys;" to help us locate the Taliban, hidden there like snakes in a garden. Even though we were given the information we asked for, extracting the enemy from the intricate maze of mud hut dwellings and alleyways was not easy, nor was it considered an issue of urgency as we presented it.

A plan was devised. The coalition forces would drop hundreds of night letters, small pamphlets, onto the sleepy village from low and slow C-130s. They fell like confetti, warning the residents that should the bad guy remain, the village would be bombed. And then we waited. Over the following days and nights, the enemy slithered away from the villages, but we were waiting in the darkness to ambush them.

Our offer to build a school had been met with warm and dignified consideration, but regrettably, they accepted our offer only for the boys. But we insisted. If they wanted a school, for their boys, then one would be built for the girls as well. They finally acquiesced. Progress began on building two schools nestled in the foothills of the Hindu Kush in a village about an hour from base camp. One for boys, and much to the chagrin of the local leadership and great dismay of the elders and other officials, one for girls. This was taken as an added insult to those in the ranks of our enemies who had managed to avoid our attacks.

The enemy waited, quietly watching from the surrounding mountains. The children filed into their respective schools, with their excited, eager little faces shining. We were proud to have made a contribution to their quality of life. But as always, we could feel eyes watching, observing, tracking our progress.

With the covertness and deftness of any wild predator, we later learned that during a school day, the members of the Taliban chained the school doors and set the buildings ablaze. The alarm sounded but it was too late. Few escaped the inferno. How does one go to sleep at night and drift off soundly? How does one go home and look at the faces of one's own children and not get destroyed inside?

This senseless tragedy only added to the hopelessness of our situation. I could not sleep but for a few minutes at a time, the sound of childish laughter and clicking pens coupled with screams all merging together in my head. A cacophony of clanging school bells shattering any peace I hoped to find. I wondered, not for the first time, if I was going mad. If my fellow service men and women were also feeling as I was, I would not know. You don't share this kind of emotion. You don't weep for lost souls. We are soldiers. We are tough. We will get even and fight back. You soldier on, in silence.

Star Power

In the aftermath of this school tragedy, we got a surprise visit from one of Hollywood's current leading actors. This was the same idea as the Bob Hope USO morale visits of yesteryear. Seldom would it be A-listers though. But this time it was Gary Sinise, who had starred in epic movies, such as *Apollo 13* and my personal favorite to this day, *Forrest Gump*. This star seemed to be keenly aware of his status and his presence was, in fact, meant as a morale booster or at least a momentary distraction for the troops. Oddly, he was not the perceived untouchable Hollywood type. We affectionately called him Lieutenant Dan (the name of the role he played in *Forrest Gump*). He was so kind and genuine. His military handlers were more uptight than he was. The Protocol/USO Office had learned a unit was coming in late from a mission outside the wire. It was not uncommon to radio ahead to the base and request extended chow time for large convoys returning late back to the camp. Mr. Sinise heard about it and he was currently waiting for his transport at the base operations and requested his detail to take him to the chow hall to greet the troops. That is how classy this guy was.

After we explained the recent school setback, and the impact it had on the hearts and minds of our troops, Mr. Sinise appeared to be emotionally moved as he wiped a tear from his eye. He listened attentively to every word and would not leave until he thanked everyone individually.

Weeks later I got a call to inform us we had a shipment being off loaded at the flight line. In haste, I barked out, "Send it over in normal distribution." "Sir," said the private on the other end of the phone, "It's two very large crates." I hung up and jumped into an SUV, and drove over to the flight line, my curiosity highly piqued.

I was faced with two gigantic, imposing, wooden crates that would require something much larger than my up-armored SUV, sent specifically to our teams to travel off base. It had to have come from one of our distinguished visitors. The boxes contained two temporary schools to be used while we had a chance to rebuild the burned down buildings!

Inside the crates we found large tents, chairs and desks—all the supplies needed, right down to chalk and paper and those darn clicking pens. My eyes blurred with tears at this enormous act of kindness. I hoped that enough children had survived to fill them.

Back in the days when I was sitting on the floor on a blanket watching *The Wonderful World of Disney*, I never imagined that "Disney" would take on a whole new meaning for me in the military. I also remember watching reruns of Bob Hope and his USO tour performances—famous people on stage, performing for the military on bases around the world. It seemed magical back then. The people seemed so happy. How could we know what was really going on?

In Afghanistan, we were lucky that the tradition continued. Star power came to the base camp every now and then—uplifting all the soldiers for a few hours and giving them motivation to continue the fight for freedom for all and to secure the safety of the United States.

One day a plane landed, nothing special, just another envoy. The passengers disembarked and headed for the protected compound. I was asked to represent our unit and greet the new arrivals. I was standing next to famous country music star Toby Keith! He arrived to do a performance for the local bases, and we were assigned to get him situated. For the first time in forever, I had a smile on my face and was happy to take on this particular duty!

For the rest of the day, people scurried about to set up a stage and create a theater-like atmosphere in the middle of nowhere. Surrounding base camps were notified and all personnel who were able, came-a-calling.

For an hour, Mr. Keith gave a patriotic, heartwarming, foot-stomping, hand-clapping performance that had everyone grinning, laughing, and enjoying themselves. Time stood still as we forgot where we were and what we were there to do. We felt appreciated as he delivered a message of thanks from a grateful nation back home. And we reveled in the combined positive energy of all the personnel who were able to attend the impromptu concert.

Show over, crowd dissipated, and Mr. Keith was on a flight out of there, right pronto. We were providing no chance for the enemy to get publicity for a celebrity victim of the Afghanistan conflict!

Beep, Beep, Beep

We were trained to follow a set of convoy and security procedures before leaving the base perimeter, which was called the "wire." I was keenly aware that these routines, if ignored, would lead to our demise. If we became complacent, took shortcuts, made missteps or forgot safety protocols, we could pay the ultimate penalty: death.

While in Afghanistan, my time spent outside the wire increased. We were very busy overseeing multiple projects in villages near the base—the hearts and minds part of the war. Convoys of our trucks would slowly advance down the dusty road into the unknown each day. There was an invisible bubble around us, evidenced by a steady beep in the helmet or the cab of the vehicle. We became so accustomed to it that it was no more noticed than our heartbeats.

Advancing mindlessly across the open plain, like so many ants in formation, the mountains encircled us in their menacing embrace. Without anything but an increase in this frantic beeping as a scant warning, a truck behind or before us could explode. Not with the sudden pop and swoosh of a goat in the minefields, rather, in a ball of fire, with flying shrapnel and shattered glass. The person with whom you just ate lunch would be gone; at times remnants of them burning or scattered in the mayhem. It is human nature to take flight, to find cover, but we had to ignore our instinct to survive, and we were tasked to fight the elusive, fearless enemy nestled above us in the ancient mountain range.

I am strong and have tap danced around many situations throughout my entire life, hiding as a gay person. I felt I could manage anything life threw at me. I DID manage anything life presented. PTSD was nothing but a thing I shrugged off to myself—nothing compared to my everyday life. I never took it seriously, but I made sure everyone else was seeing the doc or chaplain services. It never occurred to me that I should have seen someone as well.

Exit the Theater

During my first tour, I had seen the result of air reconnaissance and ground troop forays through the lens of my camera and was mostly restricted to base. But on my second tour, I witnessed the carnage firsthand, since I was outside the wire almost daily. In order to survive, I had to amputate some part of my psyche. On the outside, I was unblemished by the war, but inside I was disintegrating. Fast!

Little things started to annoy me. My judgment became impaired. In an emergency, my adrenaline would kick in and I could function, but in the wake of these episodes, I was depleted. I couldn't concentrate, couldn't sleep. Routine duties became a huge, painful chore, every day. My anger was the only emotion left at my disposal, the rest eluded me.

During my brief interruption from the war, with a quick return home to the States for the "family emergency" and then official duty at Fort Bragg, I got into an argument with a colonel at the Pentagon. She was taking me to task that not enough "good news" stories were coming from the theater of operations. This was an argument I was ready for since my first deployment. She was basically implying that I was not doing my job or doing it well. Mind you, as a reservist she filled in for the active duty that would deploy, and she had never deployed. Her criticism kind of chapped my ass since I was on my second deployment. Furthermore, this deployment was in support of the Army, so technically, I was not reporting directly to the Air Force. It was a very complex and confusing chain of command. Needless to say, I lost it. The night before I left Fort Bragg, North Carolina, to return to the war, I fired off an inappropriate e-mail out of anger. It was certainly out of character for good ol' Captain Gibson rounding nineteen years of service to the Air Force with a stellar record. I boarded the plane and left to return to Bagram, in Afghanistan, where the news of my e-mail fight with a colonel had preceded me. She was not having it and was out for blood.

After completing just seven of my eight scheduled months of deployment, things really got out of control. I was on a collision course with severe PTSD after what I experienced during both tours in Afghanistan. In the end, I left Afghanistan on not-so-favorable terms resulting from the e-mail battle with the colonel. While my Air Force supervisor was shocked and concerned for my well-being, and thought the e-mail argument was ridiculous, the colonel outranked him. Captain Gibson was wrong and, regardless, it was insubordination. That was it, cut and dry. I was sent home a month early to face a formal reprimand.

I never really came to grips with what happened during that argument. But what was done was done. I put the disciplinary problems behind me, made a decision to give up the chance to make major, and decided to retire with some humility.

It was sad actually, that a super successful career was ending with not even so much as a celebratory dinner or ceremony. To be honest, I was not in the frame of mind to have one anyway. I wanted the wounds of war to scab over, and departing the military, stage left, quietly, was the best way.

Hitting Target

When I returned home the first thing I had to do was sell my cottage house. As I listed it as fully furnished, it didn't take long to sell. I wanted to start fresh.

I had few personal belongings and moved into a new loft apartment that was partially furnished with a bed, sofa, chairs, etc. The loft was in an old refurbished cotton mill on the outskirts of Columbia, so I still made that drive to and from Sumter to report to the base. I signed a month-to-month lease to run out the clock on my twenty years of military service while I completed the series of appointments. It was a great place, with exposed bricks and beams with high ceilings and floor-to-ceiling windows on two walls since it was the largest corner unit on the top floor. Very penthouse(ish).

I was taking some time to try to relax and enjoy my new luxury loft condo. My justification was that this extravagance was a treat to myself for leaving Afghanistan alive, even if it was on unfavorable terms. It was a most expensive way to live large until retirement.

I needed a few things for the new loft and, after running a few miles, I showered and changed, and set off to knock out some serious retail therapy. I loved the feeling of being in Target—the brightness of the store, the cleanliness, the size of the open aisles, and the selection of items.

It was an unseasonably warm spring day. Dressed in flip-flops, cargo shorts, and a T-shirt (neatly pressed of course), away I went. I got to the better side of town to find my favorite Target with a Starbucks in the front of the store. "A caramel macchiato will accompany me nicely while I shop," I thought, smiling to myself as I felt the warm sweetness slide down my throat.

Grabbing a shopping cart, jolted with caffeine energy, I headed to the men's section. My standard Target routine was to peruse the clearance rack then novelty T-shirts. Most of the time I wore military-assigned apparel, so off-duty attire should be fun and would speak to who I was away from the uniform.

Barely halfway through the clearance rack, I felt sick to my stomach. At first I thought it might be the rush of sugar and caffeine after an intense, hard run. I stopped moving, sipped on my bottled water, and took a few deep breaths. I'm going to be okay, I assured myself.

Then I began to feel sweat dripping down my back and along my forehead. The store lights began caving in and flowing in and out in odd patterns, and I felt like I was suffocating! The noise in my head brought me back to the Hindu Kush with images of wartime action, exploding bodies and goats and vehicles—flashing through my head, in front of my eyes. This was a horror film or nightmare that I could not wake up from! I knew I was in trouble. I knew I had to get out. I needed AIR! I was only in the middle of the store, but the exit doors seemed miles away.

I remember stumbling my way out of the store, only able to stand by ping-ponging from clothing rack to clothing rack, grasping my head and chest. Hangers pinged off me and the racks like bullets bouncing off the Humvee. Clothing tumbled to the floor as I grasped for balance. I HAD to get out of that store. It felt like my life depended on it!

The sharp beeps in my head got progressively louder, calling to mind the blue force tracker inside the cab of the Humvee in the war zone. The subliminal beeps were getting faster. Danger was imminent. Fight or flight. Fight or flight! I wanted to flee. I needed to flee. I could not see the enemy. My heart was beating uncontrollably. I could not feel my legs. Tears were streaming down my face. I could not focus. I thought I was going to vomit.

When I finally surged out of the store into the sunshine, like a man crossing a desert without water who suddenly comes over a sand dune and finds himself in front of a water oasis, I was able to make it to a cement bumper in the parking lot, only three cars down from my car, where I finally collapsed to the ground. I honestly could not have made it all the way to my car. I sat on the bumper, put my weary, sweating head between my knees and tried to breathe. As I came back into awareness, people were pointing and staring. I began to smell something overly sweet. I realized somewhere along the escape route I had spilled the sweet coffee drink down the front of my shirt, all over my shorts and into my flip-flops which were now sticky.

"Captain Gibson, are you okay?" I heard a voice in the distance.

"Captain Gibson, can you hear me?" said a man stooping in front of me. I looked up from my coffee-stained apparel to find a fellow officer from the base and his wife looking worriedly down at me. They were more than an hour from the base! It so happened they were on a similar Target shopping retreat and noticed me in distress.

Brian helped me up and held me steady while Tammy immediately started patting my shirt dry with Kleenex from her purse in a motherly fashion. In response to his questions, I told Brian that I didn't know what was wrong.

On the front seat of my car I happened to have had a folder with notes from Dr. Reynolds, my doctor from the base. My doctor and I were honest with each other, within the constraints of the Don't Ask, Don't Tell policy. While I was never really able to bring my true identity to the table for nearly twenty years, there was something about Dr. Reynolds that assured me I could trust him from the first time I met him. It was his name on a referral document in that folder to go to the Mental Health Office. It had been my intention to get some help for anxiety. With Brian's help, we were able to locate the Mental Health Office from the base operator. I left my number and then I called my doctor.

Dr. Reynolds answered on the second ring. "Doc, it's Mark. I think I am having a heart attack or something." I told him I was with another officer from the base. The doctor asked to speak to Brian, and the next thing I knew, I was in the emergency room. I honestly don't remember getting there, but within what seemed like minutes, my doctor was at my side. My doc and his wife drove the hour from Sumter to Columbia to be with me!

I was receiving an IV drip for dehydration, as a gallon of sweat must have poured off me just trying to get out of the store. My heart rate was irregular and I was still nauseous.

Dr. Reynolds asked me to talk him through the incident. As I was explaining what happened, what I was feeling in my body and what I heard, I became nauseous because I smelled sulfur and freshly fired munitions. I got very serious and intense remembering the sensations of what I had just gone through. Doc could sense I was getting agitated again so he took my hand and rubbed my arm to reassure me I was safe as I finished relaying the story.

Apparently, I was suffering from PTSD. The barcode scanners at Target emit a beep as the items are rung through the cash register, and that noise was similar, in my subconscious mind at least, to the beeping sounds of blue force tracker that played in the Humvee and up-armored vehicles when we were moving in Afghanistan. In the theater, that sound was subliminal and the physiological response was a heightened fight-or-flight reaction in my adrenal glands. Being recently deployed, my mind was still stuck in fight mode in Afghanistan where I had been running full throttle. My body was stuck in overdrive. Despite being in Target (was my favorite store using a bullseye as its logo some kind of message?) on a sunny day in America, I could not shut down the machine.

Euromark

When I came home to South Carolina, I had completed about nineteen years and two months of service, and I would have needed just another eight months to make twenty years. So I decided to retire—without a lot of fanfare. "Now what?" I asked myself.

At a loss for what to do once I left the military, knowing that I was not capable of interacting with people in a professional manner, and really needing to recover from the battles being relived in my mind every time I closed my eyes, I decided it was a good time to go back to Europe to visit the places I had only seen briefly on the way to deployments.

When you're deployed, you get ten days off (a free vacation that isn't charged against your leave) and the military will fly you anywhere in the world that you want to go. You pick an area, and the military will get you to their hub closest to that destination. On my deployment, I took my free ticket and flew into England and then from England, I took care of my own European travel.

I visited France, metaphorically threw my ex-boyfriend Terry off the Eiffel Tower, and moved on. I knew that after retirement I wanted to go back because ten days just wasn't enough to see and experience all there was.

Now that I was a retired officer, with a pension, no expenses at home to speak of, no relationship to tie me down (or lift me up), I reconnected with my friend and former coworker, Brenda. I knew she was stationed in the Netherlands.

Brenda was stationed in Maastricht, the Netherlands, near the border of Belgium and Germany. She invited me to come visit and stay with her. I flew into the Antwerp, Belgium, airport and Brenda had made arrangements for a car service to pick me up. I felt like such a big shot. She let me use her place as my home base. And from there I went to different countries. I planned different trips. Most of them were by myself.

I got to Maastricht with a schedule of planned, three-day trips. I came bearing tons of lavish gifts for Brenda, plus I had a whole bunch of stuff shipped over there. From Maastricht, I went back to France. I went to Italy, Greece, Hungary, Poland, and the Czech Republic.

I embraced the backpacking style (and budget) trip—without the actual backpacking. I stayed in upscale hostels and traveled as my whims took me from place to place with no rush to do or see anything in particular, no one else's schedule to follow. I replaced the powdered food and reconstituted beef I had been eating for years in the military with glorious, fresh, unique, tasty, local cuisine. And I visited many pubs and cafés where I consumed lots and lots of alcohol while having delightful carefree conversations with people that knew nothing about war. All of this was a great diversion, but sadly, it did not eliminate my PTSD.

Throughout my life, I have found that when I am alone, I am often drawn to all types of music. In Europe, I was curious to find venues that had local bands playing in squares or restaurants. That was my thing. I compare it to how people collect matches or coasters from different restaurants. I did a whole season of traveling in Europe and I would go out to clubs and collect CDs as my mementos. I still have most of those CDs.

In some ways, I did find myself in Europe. I realized that it's okay for me to have a preference as to where I want to go, what I want to eat, what music I prefer, and so on. I always subverted my interests in favor of what others wanted. That need to be accepted and liked was so strong. Now that I was on my own, I became more confident to ask for what I need and want.

There were experiences and places in Europe I thoroughly enjoyed, but I didn't enjoy being alone and experiencing things by myself. I'm outgoing, but in an unfamiliar setting, I became more reclusive. At the hostels I met people from all over the world and that was somewhat uplifting, but everyone had their own agenda with places to go and things to do. In the end, they all moved on.

Brenda joined me on a couple of trips, but she was having issues with her own PTSD. Like me, she served in Afghanistan, plus she had served in Iraq, and Bosnia and Herzegovina, where she had seen a lot of death and dying. On top of it all, I wasn't paying attention to the signs. Brenda apparently thought my visit to stay with her meant that I was heading back into the role of decoy husband or boyfriend—but without the sex.

When I got to Poland, I did a lot of touristy things. I am Polish by heritage, so I wanted to learn about my culture and history. But with the sadness of being alone, I did not want to go to Auschwitz or the other concentration camps. I was staying at a B&B and the older woman who served as my hostess didn't speak English. So with the help of a housekeeper who translated for her, she guided my itinerary and insisted that I go to Auschwitz.

I went and toured the crystal factory that she recommended and some other must-see places on her list. But she still insisted I go to Auschwitz.

My B&B hostess was a Polish Jewish woman, and it seemed to be her mission in life to encourage as many people she could meet to visit Auschwitz—so that we would never forget. The old woman was probably in her eighties and I was in my late thirties. She could see that generationally, we were getting further and further away from the severity of what happened in the 1940s. Out of respect for my kind hostess, I finally agreed to go. A car came to pick me up and took me to the tour bus station.

I'm glad I went, but it was definitely emotional. It just smacks you; hits you out of the blue. The whole place is so overwhelmingly sad. There's a hush as people respectfully move slowly and quietly through the exhibits. I didn't know if I would be able to get through the tour. At certain stops, I was overcome and tears rolled down my cheek. I was not alone. Looking at the various piles of eyeglasses taken, the shoes of prisoners, the luggage, and personal items (hair brushes, mirrors, shaving equipment, toothbrushes, etc.) was so difficult. The train car that held hundreds of people crammed in as they were delivered to this extermination site. The gas chambers and dormitories where hundreds of thousands of people were imprisoned—it was so much to take in. It was too much. I think my brain was saying, "Seriously, how much more can we take up here?"

The tour guide's grandfather had died in the camp, he told us. The guide was born in a little town near Auschwitz, which is why he volunteered to take people through the camp. He leads the tours for the same reason my hostess had it posted at my B&B in Krakow, "Never forget."

It was hard to explore my personal feelings after experiencing massive devastation. But I quickly discovered that just as Europe's history was drastically different from that of the United States, so was the gay scene. I had to learn new etiquette. The gay culture throughout Europe, in most places, was surprisingly progressive. People all over were very accepting of the gay population—not just in the bars. In general, I could tell that culture had evolved to a comfortable place that I even considered that if I wanted to be an out gay person, and stopped working in the world surrounding the military, I might consider living in Europe.

On one of my trips going back to Maastricht, I felt pressure. Brenda, the "house girlfriend" was putting demands on me. I wasn't looking for demands—I had just retired. Our relationship on this trip was becoming strained, as she expected me to act as her partner in social and business situations. She treated me like her house husband, sometimes like a manservant! She expected kindnesses and special attention, and ordered me to do household chores, leaving me lists with "have dinner ready when I come home" kind of things. When she got insistent, I packed up and booked a flight home.

One of the difficulties in my life, in relationships, because of the nuances or the parameters, was to delineate between my own voice and that of my partner. Could I have an opinion that wasn't the popular one in the relationship? Could I speak my own truth or was I going to bury my own thoughts, desires, and ambitions to accommodate someone else so that they would like or love me? Or, more importantly for me, not "out" me to the military?

All my adult life, people like Brenda were able to manipulate me. I felt that since Brenda knew my secrets, she had the power to manipulate the friendship in such a way that would benefit her because I wouldn't do anything to rock the boat, because of "the secret." And people like Brenda could hold my secret against me to get what they wanted. And I let it happen, which exacerbated the "less than" way of life in my own mind.

In the past, if I didn't cooperate and act like the boyfriend or the husband, or whatever, then I might be outed. My truth would be revealed and I would pay the consequences. That's a harsh way to maintain any friendship. Can you even call that a friendship? I used to. Not anymore.

At the same time I was deciding I'd had enough of Europe, I received an interesting offer. When I first started the retirement process, I had been courted by a retired Air Force general for a corporate job. At that time, a new job was the furthest thing from my mind. I didn't want another full-time responsibility. I was just retired from THE job. My mind was a mess. I wanted to be free. I didn't want to be back in a power structure situation again with rules and regulations. But truthfully, I was only thirty-eight years old. It was cool to be that young and to be fully retired with no bills, a pension, and medical benefits. I didn't really know what I wanted to do. I didn't have a solid plan. But I realized that bumming around Europe or traveling on my own was not really how I wanted to spend the rest of my days or the rest of my resources.

The General kept hounding me to join him at Booz Allen Hamilton (BAH), a top-notch consulting firm in the Northern Virginia-D.C. area. When I got to one of the legs on my return trip, I think I was in Amsterdam, I said I would take an interview. What could it hurt?

I had to buy admission to the Delta Sky Miles lounge at the airport so I could find someplace quiet to have a Skype interview for BAH. The lady who interviewed me said, "This is a first," referring to interviewing somebody on vacation and traveling Europe. But needless to say, I got an incredible offer from them—more money than being in the military as a captain would ever have provided. And so I headed back to the U.S. and back to reality with a new plan.

Corporate Closet

Moving back to the United States from Europe, with a fabulous job waiting for me, was very different because I was wearing a whole new uniform, watching a whole new set of videos, and had different music to dance to. Yet I actually was not out at work (at BAH), because I was a military officer after all. I was recruited to the job through a general and I was working on a project that was meant to appeal to the military. So back in the closet I went, only this time the door was slightly ajar.

From day one, I knew Booz Allen Hamilton was not a good fit. I never felt welcomed there. The team I was placed on was entrenched in government contracts that seemed like a waste of money to me. I recognized that I was just not ready for the corporate, nine-to-five world.

But I was really, really good at what I did. I was still a high-functioning, optimistic, results-driven individual. But my body was like termites eating away at the inside of wood on a building. On the outside, everything looks normal, but one day, when the termites got through the core, the whole building would collapse. My body was collapsing. I was not sleeping and I began to have medical issues that were the residual effects of non-stop alcohol, lack of sleep, and PTSD. My drinking was eating away at my insides, but I could not stop. I was afraid of what I would have to really look at and deal with.

I looked at my options and found one in Costa Rica. The General encouraged me to go on a vacation and rest before making any harsh decisions or ones I would regret.

Paradise Lost

A family friend had a boss—a gay man named Henry, who was retired and living in Costa Rica. They hooked me up with him via e-mail and we became fast friends, e-mail pals. I was very interested in learning more about vacationing and possibly moving there. I was getting good at selling fully-furnished houses so I knew I could do it again. I set my sights on Costa Rica and away I flew into a dream world, my physical world seeming more like a bad dream from which I could not awaken.

Costa Rica was paradise. The ocean was beautiful. The scenery was beautiful. The men were beautiful. As I had hoped, my vacation turned into a permanent solution. I went back to northern Virginia, resigned from BAH, and departed for Costa Rica to live full-time.

My dog Gena and I moved into a simple apartment in a retirement community full of wildly colorful ex-pats. Drinking, dancing, partying was a way of life. But between parties, when left alone, sadness hung like a gray cloud around my head; it was emptiness that came from lacking purpose.

I got involved with a local animal welfare organization SASY (Stop Animal Suffering, Yes!) and I threw myself into volunteering. I met Angelica, one of the founding organizers, and we quickly became friends. Life got a little less lonely.

One day, while sitting at a local bar, I overheard the man next to me telling a story about a house he owned up in the mountains. It was, he said, just like the glass house created for the movie *Sleeping with the Enemy*. The original house was in Cape Cod, Massachusetts, and he was looking to sell the replica. I interrupted and asked him to tell me more about it.

Apparently, this gentleman was a Dutch architect and had designed and built the house for someone who retired in Costa Rica. The purchaser had then declared bankruptcy and, voilà, the house was back in the possession of the architect. Sight unseen (I knew the house from the movie!), I offered to buy the house. Every penny I had saved went into purchasing this house at the top of the mountain. He did insist that I go look at the house with him, so we grabbed our drinks and away we went. He had a Mercedes 4x4, built like a Sherman tank. We needed it to get up the steep incline and then descend back down to the goat trail to a cliff where this house was located. Again, once I saw the view, I said I would buy before ever setting foot into the house. After I walked into the house it was equally as impressive as the view. "I'll take it!" I confirmed.

The first time I tried to drive my small SUV (I named her Renee) up to the house, I realized just how remote this place was. The "road" was nothing more than a worn-down path of jagged rocks, sand, mud, potholes, and small stones. I should have purchased a helicopter but, financially unfeasible, I put my car on Craigslist to sell. I started looking for something sturdier to make it up that mountainside as the rainy season was coming.

A woman named Joy responded to my listing. When she and her husband came to meet me and test drive the car, Joy and I clicked and became instant friends. Her husband was smoking HOT—I tried not to stare. The three of us hit it off instantly with the military being something we had in common. She was a fabulously successful and stylish American businesswoman with her foreign headquarters in Costa Rica and her U.S. headquarters outside Atlanta. She was kind, but tough as an old boot and wielded a wicked, dry, sense of humor.

I wanted so much to stay in her orbit that I told them I wouldn't sell them my car! What if my car broke down and they resented me? Joy, being practical, wrote me a note that said she guaranteed to remain friends with me no matter what happened with the car. She kept the car a long time and we are still friends!

Joy's husband lived in the United States and commuted between the two countries. I often spent time in Joy's house in the central valley of Costa Rica, just outside the capital city of San José, while her husband was away. Her sixteen-year-old son was in school and I would keep Joy company. We'd shop, dine out, and go to events. Sometimes, when the phone would ring I'd answer, "Gay House Husband." When her "real" husband would call, he'd hear my greeting and would burst into laughter. I think he was happy to have an ex-military guy watching over his family, knowing that there was absolutely no threat of losing his wife to me!

Meanwhile, I met Juan through some friends. He was ready to move in with me from the beginning! I was his ticket out. Juan found a well-traveled, older, financially secure ex-pat to be his entrée into a society where dinner included cocktail hour, hors d'oeuvres, seating cards, and wine with each course. This was definitely an older-younger romantic, flirty relationship, but nothing long term was ever in my mind. Gay Tico men, if they were the only son, would never leave their families. It was their culture. I was safe.

Yes, Gena, my Jack Russell Terrier, came with me to our new home in Costa Rica. She was very well behaved, although she got a little crazy when she saw squirrels, monkeys, or anything that moved in our yard. In Costa Rica, she chased birds and parakeets, squirrels, and lots of other little critters.

Angelica, from SASY, convinced me that I needed more protection for my home. So, against my true wishes, I adopted a Rottweiler named Rufus. Naturally, Rufus and I bonded the minute we met, and all hesitation went out of my heart! Rufus, my outdoor dog and home protector, became my confidant. In the evenings, sitting on the veranda enjoying the fragrant rainforest breeze and listening to music with a glass of wine or vodka in my hand, I would talk on and on to Rufus. He was with me for endless tropical days and nights, listening to my increasingly drunken verbal wanderings while Gena and Juan flitted about, happy as moons in orbit, inside the glass box.

We lived in a picture-perfect area. It was, nonetheless, vulnerable to the poverty that was only ever at arm's length. Gangs of Nicaraguan bandits would case remote domiciles in the higher elevations. Since most of the residents had guard dogs for protection, they'd developed a cruel and effective remedy to remove these canine impediments by poisoning hot dogs and throwing them over the fence. It wasn't long before I came home to find my beloved companion Rufus terminally ill from this prank. I was heartbroken, and tried to nurse Rufus back to health. I just couldn't bear the thought of another being that I was close to leaving me. But he did.

My drinking became suicidal. I was constantly in a fog that would descend into blackouts. These blackouts were both merciless and merciful. Merciless in that they rendered me powerless to control my life, but merciful in that they washed away the pain I could no longer control.

My deterioration into oblivion was progressive. One morning Juan found me facedown in a puddle of blood on the marble floor of the shower, having just missed the glass divider between the shower and toilet—a half wall of glass.

The floating infinity staircase in my *Sleeping with the Enemy* house had no railing. One night I'd fallen, landing facedown on the Italian marble floor. I remember waking to excruciating pain in my shoulder, and wondering what had happened and where all the blood had come from. Surmising that it was from me, I was able to load Gena into the Jeep, and managed to drive myself up the steep mountain, holding my breath in pain, reaching over with my left hand to shift gears, thinking all along that I was going to pass out from the pain and the car would go careening backward and kill me and Gena!

I arrived at Angelica's house to leave Gena. Angelica was the only person with whom I would entrust Gena. Angelica was horrified when I arrived looking like I had been in a terrible auto accident. She knew this was a result of drinking and gently took in my shaking dog and looked at me with sad disappointment and disgust, "*Oh, Mark.*" I left and drove myself to the hospital.

I don't remember much after getting to the hospital other than the surgeon being very concerned with my blood work. But I was in so much pain, and thanks to good vital signs, we went ahead with the surgery and a full shoulder replacement. The fall had shattered the bones in my shoulder.

When I finally came to, I was in a dark, cold, private room. There was a hazy visage of a person sitting in the room at the foot of the bed. I didn't know where I was. I remember thinking it was odd I was not wearing any underwear. I tried to get up, and must have let out a yelp as I moved my right arm. The nurse came in, *poof!* the image at the foot of my bed was gone, and I was struggling to get up. The nurse was forcefully insisting in Spanish that I remain in bed. She sedated me, which took hold fast as I dozed off into drugged slumber.

The next time I woke, as I slowly opened my eyes, I saw Juan was at my bedside. I had never seen someone look so scared. He wept, as I was still lacking the understanding of the severity of what had occurred. Somehow Juan was able to reach Joy by e-mail, as he did not have an international phone. Joy, who had been in the States, came to my bedside at once.

Without judgment, but extreme fear and concern, Joy volunteered to be my health proxy and get me out of the hospital. Everyone spoke Spanish and between her and Juan they helped me process out.

Joy picked me up from the hospital and, like a dumbass, I wanted to go to the liquor store, get my dog, and go home to the glass house in the mountains. Joy took me to retrieve my dog, but convinced me to stay with her in the valley so she and her son could help take care of me, at least until I got some movement back in my shoulder. I was a stubborn old drunk, but Joy knew how to word it like it was my idea. She let me bring my dog and camp out on her sofa.

And yet, despite everything that warned me to stop, I just kept on drinking. The doctors told me if I continued to drink I would die. They weren't telling me anything I didn't already know. Blood in my urine, kidneys failing...after all, wasn't that the plan?

Once I was able to sit up, I would Skype Mom from time to time and make sure the glass of wine or vodka would be off camera (did I think she was an idiot?).

"Are you TRYING to kill yourself?" she sobbed. "I don't understand. You have such a bright future and you are killing yourself, can't you see it?" I could. I could see it. But I couldn't tell her that.

"Please, Mark! Please try and get some help!" she whimpered as we hung up the phone. This was upsetting enough for me to mention the call to Joy.

Glass of wine in hand, back at my glass house, I sat on my veranda, over-looking the central valley high atop the village of Escazu outside the capital of San José, as I contemplated my mother's pleas. I could see the inactive vol-canoes off in the distance. It was a balmy evening, the breeze was strong, the thick, burgundy room-darkening shades were flapping. Endless days turned to endless nights. At this point I measured the hours by numbers of bottles of wine or vodka.

One would think that after blacking out, breaking bones, waking up cov-ered in blood, and being rushed into emergency surgery that I would have hit bottom. Nope. My body was like a machine. I healed quickly and was already an expert on combining pain meds with vodka for an extra special high.

My body recovered as time went on, but I was never to regain full strength or mobility in my right arm. I felt alone, hopeless, and trapped in a dark hole, comforted only by my growing addiction to painkillers.

Sober Awakening

Sleeping (or should I say passing out?) was an issue for me. I would drift off in early evening after a long day of drinking. Once my body began to feel withdrawal, I would stir and wake. I used to love to sit for hours, sipping some concoction of wine and ginger ale to make it last longer and look out over the valley at all of the lights. It seemed calming to me. It made the chatter in my head drift away or at least be held at bay.

One night I remember just hovering near sleep, and hearing the Mac computer in the office chime for new mail. I typically did not hear these chimes, but my phone simultaneously let me know of a new e-mail. I stumbled out of bed onto the cool Italian marble floors, in a slumber-haze, and made my way down the hall to the office. I moved the wireless mouse to activate the screen and woke the system from its own slumber.

I clicked on the mailbox and opened my mail. It looked like junk mail, but it was from Joy. I quickly scanned the e-mail and would have deleted it because it had words like "guaranteed," "trust us," and "money back," but Joy is one of the smartest people I know. Running a huge worldwide company, she would not take the time to send me junk. I read on. I re-read the entire message word for word; then clicked on the hyperlinks to the website. I played the videos and watched ALL of the testimonials, finding them so powerful, real, painful, sad, uplifting, and hopeful. They were not professionally produced, but they were authentic. I must have read the entire site six times as the sun was cresting over the still-sleeping volcanoes across the valley.

I crafted a short message to Joy: "I'm in."

Later that morning I remember blowing up Joy's phone with excitement. "Joy, it's Mark! Are you kidding me right now? Are you kidding me with this e-mail?! Guaranteed success over alcohol, heroin, cocaine addictions. Guaranteed or your money back?"

"That's what it says," she answered.

"Yeah, right!" I replied. Challenging their statement, "They have not met Mark Gibson, ha!" I scoffed. "Oh, and you are coming with me, I can't do this alone." I added.

Deep down inside, it was no joke! I had grown so tired of the despair and utter chaos that possessed my mind and was fueled by the alcohol. I wanted this more than I wanted anything in my life. More than my Air Force career, more than my glass house on the mountain in Costa Rica, I wanted to live. But I knew one thing was for sure—what I was experiencing, being controlled by alcohol, was not living. I wanted to breathe and live an alcohol-free life.

The treatment, which was not approved in the U.S. or in Canada at the time, involved ingesting a rare plant root from Africa. It was extremely expensive and administered by an African shaman.

"What the hell?" I thought to myself. "Money-back guarantee."

I called the number on the website and applied for a partial scholarship and hocked everything else I owned to raise enough cash to get accepted in the upcoming session. Before I knew it, I was speeding toward Liberia, Costa Rica, in the back of my old car, now Joy's car. Joy and a friend of ours were in the front seat.

The research said that ingesting this root can take you on a journey or path through existence in this space and time of life. The ladies traveling with me were going for a mind-altering experience. I was going to do battle; I was going to save my life.

The Root Cause

When the day arrived, I started to drink early out of habit and nerves. I increased total consumption heavily as we went rolling through the tropics to Liberia, swerving our way around tight curves, along death-drop cliffsides, getting drunk on boxed wine and shots of tequila.

Hiding my true self literally and figuratively as a child, led to hiding my desires in my marriage, closeting my true self in my chosen military profession, which eventually led to hiding in a bottle to numb the pain and suppress my authentic self, who was trying to claw its way out of hiding. Here I was, terrified, ready to step out into the world as my true self and hide no more. If the program worked, that is. If we didn't die careening around the mountain curves! I was thinking, that this was it, my Hail Mary pass.

This was no cheap little adventure. The treatment with the Iboga root came at a cost of several thousands of dollars, but I kept reminding myself, a 100 percent money-back guarantee. As the Spanish road signs foretold, we were getting close to our destination. I'm not sure why, but Joy (our designated driver) asked if we could stop at this one last bar. I think she wanted to double check that we all truly were ready to go through with this. I was all in; I was also very drunk. But again, it was hard to notice as I was extremely high functioning.

None of us knew what to expect when we arrived at the retreat site. It sounded so mysterious, so exotic, and because I was drunk, it also seemed a little silly.

When we arrived, the place turned out to be an impressive property. There was a very large, modern guest house in the center of the property up on a slight hill. Several small houses and buildings were scattered around the property. Everything was well kept, neat, clean, and tidy.

Finally, we approached the house where we were greeted by a handsome black man. Tall and imposing, he introduced himself in a very deep voice, as Shaman Moughenda. His accent was South African and, at times, difficult to understand. I was looking around, noting that the men were rather cute. (Yes, sometimes my priorities are a little screwed up!) There were several other people there shuffling about. Everybody was curious.

The house was nice, very clean, just not very warm or welcoming. Honestly, I had no clue who the people were or what the agenda was. I knew nothing, other than what the website said, and I put a lot of trust in Joy. I just kept thinking I had nothing to lose and everything to gain.

Some chime or sound reached us and we were all summoned to the middle house on the property, which turned out to be like a large carport. In the driveway, there was a small campfire lit, and folding chairs placed in a circle.

Soon about a dozen of us were sitting in a big circle. I mentally rolled my eyes, thinking we might break into a round of Kumbaya!

At first the conversation was light, casual, airy—getting to know you types of introductions and activities.

Shaman Moughenda asked if anyone had used today. Of course, the majority of us lied. He quietly told us in a firm but casual tone that this was *his* house with *his* rules. The only way anything was going to work here is with brutal honesty. So again, he asked and came right to me. Without skipping a beat, I said, "Hell, yes, I used today." I was drunk at that moment. He thanked me for being honest.

Off in the distance we could see the guest house. There seemed to be lots of activity in the house as shadows in the lights appeared like clothes flying in the air. I didn't really think much about it at that moment until Moughenda explained, as he pointed up to the house, that the staff searching our rooms and cars were caregivers.

We were all sobering up now and were somewhat taken aback. Meanwhile, we could hear those cute little attendants tossing our rooms, tossing our cars, ferreting out any traces of drugs or alcohol. The others that were there for the life experience felt bad for us, but it didn't affect them. Joy was a bit miffed that some staff got into her car and angered to learn I had hidden more boxed wine under the seats in the back of her car.

The attendants brought down the smuggled items and lined them up. Drugs were hidden in toothpaste and underarm deodorant, and in little Ziploc baggies. The eight boxes of wine in the contraband lineup were mine.

There were other health concerns as some people had stuffed or ingested drugs in condoms. Game on. People were escorted to bathrooms. I had to dump out the wine I brought. I had to promise there was nothing else hidden. Drugs and alcohol, hell, even soda was banned from the house. No high fructose corn syrup sugary drinks.

The shaman explained that he would be administering the Iboga root to us. We sat around talking as he encouraged us to open our minds. "I will also be taking the root," he advised. Soon he gave us all the root, taking some himself.

Nothing happened. At least not yet. My mind was racing. I came all this way and spent all this money to have some guy give me a nasty tasting root to eat and stare into the fire or lie on a mat under the stars?

One by one people were dropping like flies. It was not just scary, it was Jim Jones, Jonestown, Guyana scary at first, but oddly also calm and peaceful. Everyone had taken their root and went to the mats to relax. A little like a Woodstock mushroom or LSD trip. Not me. I felt marginally buzzed, but that was it. Having been drinking and drugging since I was fourteen years old, I obviously had a very high resistance and tolerance for both drugs and alcohol.

Just about everyone needed only one of the homemade gel capsule root pills. Then one or two needed a second one. I was on the third administered capsule and still felt nothing except exhaustion. So after a long pause I looked up at Moughenda and the staff as I bid them good night and started out for the guest house. I got up and started to walk, but it was like my legs were Jell-o. Two aids came to my rescue, one on each side, and Moughenda was standing in front of me, calmly talking to me to come over and lay down on one of the mats waiting for me. It was next to Joy's mat. She was peacefully relaxed and just watching me, smiling. I was becoming increasingly annoyed.

And then, while lying there staring at the canopy of stars overhead, I realized that I was tripping. I was as high as a kite. This meant that the shaman must be, too, but he didn't seem to be. He was walking among the mats in the dark, his deep voice and the light of his cigarette the only indication of his presence.

Over the course of the evening I'd been given several Iboga roots. Even in that state, I realized that my tolerance must be awfully high as others were puking and running to the latrines and cursing all around me. Then it hit me. I started to projectile vomit. Now I understood what the five-gallon white buckets were for. Not me though, I wanted to puke in a bathroom. One of the attendants escorted me to the bathroom. I motioned as if to close the door and he stopped me and escorted me into the small bathroom. It was getting weird and uncomfortable for me. But then realized why he was there. I began to lose control of bodily functions fast, and got very dizzy. The attendant didn't want me to fall or hurt myself. I wanted to die. It would not stop. I would try to sip water but I puked across the bathroom, on his clothes and shoes. Honest to God, I had no idea how I could puke this much, especially while sitting on the toilet. I thought it was an exorcism. The attendant stripped me down and put me in the shower. Once I stopped pushing my insides out, and I was showered and cleaned, the attendant put me in some clean, simple, cotton clothes and escorted me out to the waiting Moughenda.

"C'mon, Mark," he said as he took me by the arms. "You will be okay now. Just lay down, get your breathing under control and I will be right back." I just put my head back and looked at the sky and began focusing on breathing rhythms.

Soon Moughenda was standing over me again.

"So, how are you doing, Mark?" he asked.

"I'm good," I told him. I was not startled or nervous at all, I felt weak and very thirsty.

"What do you see?"

"I see a door."

"Go through it," he urged, but for some reason I was reluctant.

"Do I need permission?" I asked as I began knocking on the door.

"No, Mark. Just go through it!" he laughed, sauntering away into the darkness.

The door was as real to me as if it had been solid and right in front of me, made of wood or steel. In my mind, I opened the door and there before me was a lush, large green field. On the far side, at the opposite end of the field, was a bench. I could tell there was a man sitting on the bench.

The shaman was back. I told him what I saw.

"And who is that fellow?" he asked.

"I don't know. I'm afraid to approach him. I keep trying to get his attention but he won't turn around."

"Mark, stop asking permission. Go see who it is."

As I crossed the field, I felt both terror and excitement. Who could this be and why was he here? The grass was manicured and smelled fresh.

I slowly approached the bench. Looking back over my shoulder, watching the door, I made it to the front side of the bench and took another step to confront the man sitting there, in silence. I looked at the man's face. It was a familiar face and yet strange. How the hell? It was me!

"Have a seat," he said.

"What would you like to talk about?" I asked myself. He squarely faced me on the bench now and reached out to touch my arm and leg.

"Why did you do this to me?" his voice was small, and full of sorrow.

I looked into his blue eyes, those eyes I'd looked into every day in the mirror. There was such sadness, such betrayal in them. And in an instant, I knew how I'd hurt this person, myself. I felt such compassion in that moment.

Shaman Moughenda was suddenly there with us.

"How do you feel?" the shaman asked me.

We talked about my feelings. They came rushing out of me like a pent-up river, suddenly released.

"Ask him where he wants to go, Mark!"

I did.

He got up and motioned for me to go for a walk in the huge grass field, "I want to see the good and the bad."

I have no idea how long we walked and talked. It was like watching an old, familiar movie with a close friend. And as each painful memory came into view, the part of me that I'd medicated away, comforted me.

Finally, this movie seemed to end in the present moment. We were back at the door. He patted my shoulder, the bad one, as if a reminder of what I did to us.

"See you later, I am counting on you to survive," he said, smiling as he walked out of view across the field back toward the bench.

I was the last person to complete the process that night. By dawn, my eyes were yellow and I was urinating blood badly, shaking and slamming through withdrawal like a runaway train.

I felt good mentally; I just needed my body to catch up. The attendants helped me up and walked me to the car to give me a ride up to the guest-house. Which was silly to me as it was only a couple blocks to walk, but I didn't have the strength and now was not the time to be macho. Two of them physically walked me up the three short stairs into the house. I was greeted by Joy who had already showered and was waiting for me. They strongly encouraged eating some of the fresh fruit that was cut up in the kitchen to start restoring the electrolytes that had been depleted from the vomiting.

The same two attendants then physically helped me up the stairs—one in front, one in the back to get me to my room. It was very cool and there was a white, five-gallon pail next to my bed. I groaned. I just wanted to lie down. Joy had them bring another bed in the room so she could watch over me. I slowly drifted off to sleep.

I am told that I slept for twenty-four hours. I remember waking up and not really knowing where I was. I was dizzy, and that made me nauseous.

I fell down when I tried to get out of bed. My body started to go into convulsions while I was trying to get up off the floor. An attendant must have heard the thump of me falling down. At first, he could not find me because I was between the bed and the wall. I could hear him in the room, but I could not speak to let him know where I was. Then he turned on more lights and found me on the floor shaking out of control.

He came to me, held my face up to his, gently moved my hair out of my eyes and said, "Mark, can you hear me? Mark, look at me. Blink your eyes if you can hear me." I started to talk, slurred speech. Joy had returned and strong concern was reflected in her eyes. The attendant, looking scared, hurriedly went to get the shaman.

Moughenda came to check on me, took my face with both of his hands and said, "You are going to be okay, Mark; this is the detox. The Iboga root went in your body today to the time before you had your first drink. Your body is going through withdrawal and this is not uncommon. We are going to take you to the hospital to get more fluids and an IV, okay?"

Soon I was racing toward a hospital with delirium tremors, my central nervous system shutting down. My liver began to shut down, but I was somehow stabilized in the nick of time. My body hadn't been ready for this detox.

By the second day, I felt better. My ears were ringing and I found it impossible to sit still.

By day three, I was vomiting again. I was starving but couldn't keep anything down.

By day four, the results of all my lab work were back. I had nearly 90 percent liver failure. My blood work was a mess; my whole system was upside down.

During this week, I was supposed to undergo one more Iboga treatment. Unfortunately, due to my horrible blood test and liver function, Moughenda came to me and we talked very seriously about how I was not physically capable to continue with the treatment. My mind said yes and I tried to convince him to continue. I NEEDED this to work. But he would not take the risk with my body.

Moughenda got uncomfortably close to my face and stared me in the eyes and asked if I understood the severity of the situation, "If you drink again, it will kill you."

Joy again took me under her wing. She had me stay at her house while I recovered. She taught me how to eat healthy and how make powerful vegetable and fruit juice concoctions. She got me strong enough so I could go back to my glass palace.

While at Joy's place, I started eating a gluten-free diet, since she was allergic to gluten. I was eating fresh fruits and vegetables, consuming no drugs or alcohol. Day by day, I was getting my strength back and sleeping much better. I even began running again.

After a thirty-day waiting period and another blood test, I returned to the Iboga House and took three roots. It was like rebooting a computer, resetting my system. I got a little nauseous, but I didn't get sick and once I ate some fresh fruit, I felt fine.

My second trip to finish the treatment was much more psychotropic. Almost relaxing. The waking dreams were not as vivid. I was more comfortable. I imagine it was like tripping on LSD or something. I was fascinated by the stars above, the moving breezes; I felt like I was walking through the galaxy and was feeling love.

The Iboga root was taking me back to the moment before the very first beer I had with my brother at a very young age. It was resetting my central nervous system to before I was addicted.

Mark 2.0—It Wasn't Easy,
But It Was Worth It

I couldn't help remembering, how when I was eight years old, my mother had taken me to a church service at a little black Pentecostal church in Saratoga Springs, New York. I played one of the wise men in the Christmas play that year. The pastor's wife, Mama Tate, was a very wise older woman. She looked at me and she said, "Mark, one day, after you've gone through some hard times, you're gonna be alright, you're gonna be somebody."

I kept hold of the hope and promise that Mama Tate told me so many years before. Although most of my life was hidden and wrought with guilt, shame, and secrecy, I felt a sense of acceptance and vindication on December 22, 2010. It was almost a form of validation that my service to the nation I love so much mattered and for the first time since my retirement I truly felt proud to be a gay military officer, an American patriot.

"We are not a nation that says, 'Don't Ask, Don't Tell.' We are a nation that says, 'Out of many, we are one.' We are a nation that welcomes the service of every patriot. We are a nation that believes all men and women are created equal. Those are the ideals that generations have fought for. Those are the ideals we uphold today."

—*President Barack Obama at the signing ceremony of the*
Don't Ask, Don't Tell Repeal Act, December 22, 2010

• • •

It wasn't easy but it was worth it. I left my addiction, fear, guilt, and shame at the Iboga House and have been sober since 2011.

Doctors told me that I'd never live to be forty-five at the rate I was going—writing checks my body could not cash—literally drinking myself to death. After Iboga, and making a sincere apology to myself, and solid commitment to live life authentically and healthfully, Mark 2.0 was born.

The Iboga experience taught me so much, but the most important lesson I learned from Iboga was authenticity. Have you ever found it difficult to say you're sorry to a loved one and mean it? Try doing it with yourself.

The shaman and I talked about my experience afterward. The reasons it took so many doses of the Iboga root to take effect was twofold. One: I had a very strong tolerance for substances. Two: Decades of iron-clad walls that had been built up to hide secrets, and mask shame and guilt, alerted my mind to activate my body's adrenal fight or flight system. That was a lethal combination stronger than coalition forces off to war.

When I approached myself on the bench during the Iboga experience, there was a sense of profound sadness. It was real, raw, and vulnerable.

As I sat down on the bench with myself and looked out across the grassy knoll, almost as if I were completely naked, a flood of emotions whizzed through my head. Shame of course, I had perfected that along with guilt, but the most compelling was sadness that surpassed all levels of sadness I had ever felt up to that point. And if I had to pinpoint it, this would be the moment that I realized it was time to get to work and fix it—almost like a surgeon inspecting the sharpness of a scalpel. The profound sadness occurred when calm, younger-looking, healthy Mark on the bench looked up at me with piercing blue eyes and puddles of tears forming and asked me, "Why? Why did you do this to me?" One teardrop pooled enough to race down his cheek. I could not respond.

He proceeded to tell me that there was danger ahead and life as we knew it would be over. "Today and tomorrow are going to be no cakewalk either," he said in jest as he sniffled to clear his nose and wipe away the pools of tears in the bottom of his eyes. Exposed and exhausted, I took a deep breath and the only thing that came to mind was to apologize and mean it! But before you say it, understand what it means and what will have to happen in order for him to believe you.

As I sat next to myself, I put my left hand on my right shoulder as I continued to look out into the landscape. Then I apologized. Then I turned my body, looking deep into his soul and said it again. But this time, I took my hands and held my face and wiped the tears away with my thumbs and vowed, "I will never, NEVER drink again. I will never abuse you, or harm you, or take you for granted. I love you."

This was a heavy enough conversation for one visit, so we both turned to look straight ahead. I could hear our heartbeats settle down and the calmness of our breathing. Small talk led to laughter and just like that, our time together was over. I watched as he walked across the grass, turned and looked back over his right shoulder and said, "Good luck, Mark. I will see you soon."

I started back toward the door from where I entered after signaling a thumbs-up followed by a wave. It was almost like we both knew what was about to happen was not going to be pleasant or easy. But we both knew that we were going to make it to the "other" side. We had each other.

Authenticity. Like the air we breathe, this is the one constant I need in my life in order to survive. To achieve this constant:

1. I have to be brutally honest and authentic with myself and others around me each and every day. Think of this as clean oxygen. Really look at yourself in the mirror, talk to yourself. Be honest, authentic, and real.

2. Embrace change. Life and relationships are going to change. Some change for the better and some may end. It's okay. The ones that end were most likely dead on the vine; your lack of authenticity was keeping them alive.

3. Don't be so hard on yourself. This does not mean lower your standards, but damn it, be kind to yourself and celebrate the victories as intensely as you correct the defeats.

4. Master conflict management and resolution skills. These critical skills will help you stay true to yourself as you cope with, and overcome, adversity while maintaining your authenticity.
5. Love yourself. Unconditionally.

• • •

Today I realize I was trapped in a vicious cycle of inauthenticity. I'm not blaming anyone. I chose to keep my life secret. I am not blaming the government for its *Don't Ask, Don't Tell* policy. But I am trying to highlight how a policy can have devastating effects on a person's soul. It is inevitable that how you are forced to act during the day for your professional life winds up in your personal life, and in your relationships.

To this day, my only regret is getting married. It's not because I got married to a bad person. She wasn't. She was nice, innocent, and kind. Sadly, like many others in the same situation, we inadvertently involve somebody else in the misery, the charade. And it hurt a really good person who got caught in my web, and for that I am deeply sorry.

Part of rebuilding my life is to take the valuable lessons I learned and try to help others avoid the pain I was lucky enough to survive. My mission now is to help other people find their own true self and to live authentically to avoid the death spiral that brought me so close to the end of my story. I volunteer for programs I believe in. I work to empower young people going through challenges similar to the ones I faced in my youth, to stand up, take charge of their own lives—to be fully themselves.

So many people hide, and in the hiding, they suffer and harm themselves in deep, soul-crushing ways. My journey began with hiding my bed-wetting, then covering my sexuality, which led to crippling low self-worth, hidden behind a jovial, can-do overachieving façade, pressed into a lifelong addiction to numbing alcoholism and dysfunctional relationships.

No one should die (emotionally or physically) because they cannot live their truth:

- Whether you were abused as a child or find yourself living in an abusive relationship.
- If you are suffering under the weight of religious oppression and regulations.
- If you are wrestling with PTSD or a traumatic loss.
- If you are struggling to accept your sexuality and, in my case, homosexuality.
- Plagued with drug or alcohol addiction.
- Or for whatever reason you have *Served in Silence*.

Living your life in segments, as I did, pretending to be one thing to family, another to work, another to friends, results in living an inauthentic life. Hiding my secrets (and others' secrets, too) was a horrible way to live. I felt like I was under the guillotine all the time, waiting for the blade to drop. But today I am an atom spinning through this universe, doing the dance of life. And I'm alright. You will be, too.

Whether you seek to find your authenticity with the assistance of someone else in a relationship or on your own, I believe you truly cannot achieve authenticity until you have an authentic relationship with yourself.

May your journey lead you to reaching your true authentic self to dance, laugh, and love like it is going out of style, breaking whatever chains that cause you to serve in silence.

I promise you that once you truly love yourself authentically, the doors will open to unimaginable happiness, joy, prosperity, and success. Live on!

#LiveAuthentically

Captain Mark David Gibson, north of Kabul, Afghanistan, 2006

Running the Golden Gate Bridge, 2014

Singing and dancing in 2015 with my lifelong hero and inspiration,
the incomparable Ms. Patti LaBelle

With Aaron Borrelli (a.k.a. Mr. Wonderful) in 2018

Acknowledgments

I would like to thank and acknowledge my incredible team at Publish Your Purpose (PYP) Press for believing in me and guiding me through this process. Jenn, Lisa, Heather, Niki, and Fern—each of you has made a deep and profound impact on my life, and for that I am most appreciative and thankful. From Spark to Ignite to Flame to Launch, it was one hell of a ride!

Gail Moore, we did it! Thank you from the bottom of my heart for believing in me and getting this party started. Your counsel, guidance, and friendship has always been a beacon of hope throughout my life.

Thank you, Sam McClure, Senior Vice President, National Gay & Lesbian Chamber of Commerce®, for the introduction to Jenn T. Grace, PYP Press. Sam, your solid leadership and friendship over the years have been a cornerstone in guiding, mentoring, and challenging me to live bolder, brighter, and more intentionally as a professional gay man. You have changed my life by helping me shed light on Mark 2.0—authenticity reimagined.

To Mr. Eugene Cornelius Jr.: Thank you, sir, for believing in me and allowing me to live my true authentic self professionally at the U.S. Small Business Administration. When you were tasked by President Obama to help the federal government consider ways to be more inclusive to the LGBT Community, it was my distinct honor to put the wind at the sails of your

Many Faces One Dream tour and LGBT Business Builder. The absolute high-light of my professional career.

I owe a tremendous amount of gratitude to David W. Perry, who also paved the way to encourage authenticity on the job. Truly one of the best bosses a renegade maverick could possibly have.

To Ms. Patti LaBelle, in my darkest hours your music has inspired me to find a better place *Somewhere Over the Rainbow.* With songs like: *On my Own, Oh People, When you've Been Blessed* and so many more, your music has soothed my soul and helped me mend crushing painful wounds of war and silence. Your voice has broken the sound barrier in my closet many times for decades and helped me find a *New Attitude.* With kind regards, and adoration. *You Are My Friend!*

To my Costa Rica friends, angels on earth who saved my life—there are simply no words to express my feelings and emotions. Harmony, Johnny, Lili, Win, Sydelle, George, Francesca, Judy, and Rita: I made it.

Johnny G., you never turned your back on me or our friendship. We made it through the rain. Thank you for all of your advice and leadership over the years. You taught me how to plant the seeds of authenticity during the most troubling of times.

To my Air Force/military family: Regardless of serving in silence with you, I would do it all over again, this time more authentically. Each of you are the true spirit of America that makes up the fabric of our patriotic heritage. I am humbled and honored to have served with each and every one of you. I salute you.

To my Texas connection, my center of gravity (Bryn, Christopher, Suzanne, Pam, Mark & Carolyn, and Phyllis & Richard): I have always found my way "home" to the open arms of Texas and the Silver Dollar & C-Bar Ranches during times of trouble, turmoil, triumph, accomplishment, and love. Each visit is better than the last to rest, recharge, mend wounds, and drive on. Suzanne, you are my hero. Bryn, I aspire to achieve your steadfast loyalty, honor, and integrity. I honestly do not know where I would be today without you.

I could not be here today without the love and support of my parents—Mom always encouraging me to have balance in my life, and Dad and Lynn living the example of respect, honesty, and integrity. I am honored to be your son and I love you very much.

To my brothers and sister: I know it has not been easy having a brother like me, and for that I apologize. It was not your choice that I chose to live a life "Served in Silence." You have each taught me so much along the way, and for that I am grateful. I am excited for honest and authentic relationships in the future.

Special thanks to my circle of friends and neighbors in Midtown Atlanta, Savannah, and Lake Oconee, my consummate cheerleaders and support system. Thank you for always encouraging and believing in me. I value our deep, rewarding friendships.

Aaron, you are not only my Mr. Wonderful, my "somekindafantastic," you are my heart. Thank you for encouraging, supporting, and pushing me on this project we call life and love. You encompass every facet of the definition of "partner" and for that, I thank you and love you with all of my heart. Excited for what is next in the "upside down." I 4 U, Me

Lastly, to you, Mark David Gibson: I am proud of you. I am immensely sorry and promise I will never hurt you or let you down again. I love you, Mark!—What's next?

About the Author

J ust a small-town boy from upstate New York, the best was yet to come. Retired U.S. Air Force Captain Mark David Gibson, like many other young people lost and searching, joined the military as a "ticket out" to find himself and see the world. The strict structure of the military was the perfect solution for harnessing this young person's scattered energy, poor life choices, and dangerous decisions. Despite a life foundation built on shifting sands of denial, secrecy, shame, and guilt, Mark found a place to call home in the Air Force.

Photo: Tyler Ogburn

Long before Don't Ask, Don't Tell became an official policy, it was an unwritten rule invented and perfected as the accepted way of life for young Mark.

Gibson, a twenty-year, highly decorated war veteran served ten years enlisted, took an educational break in service, and then served ten more years as a Public Affairs Officer. He deployed multiple times to Southwest Asia in support of Operations Enduring Freedom and Noble Eagle.

During an educational break in service, Mark's determination and overachieving ambition was demonstrated by acquiring bachelor's and master's degrees simultaneously and earning a commission in the Air Force as an

Officer, while working part-time to become the number one salesperson for Bose Corporation in Framingham, Massachusetts.

After retirement from the Air Force and a short backpacking respite through Europe, Mark tried his hand in the corporate world. He landed a highly prized, prestigious position as a consultant in Washington, D.C., only to learn he did not mesh well with the corporate "dog-eat-dog" world. Mark then retired to Costa Rica with his beloved Jack Russell Terrier, Gena.

Costa Rica would prove to save Mark's life, helping him successfully conquer severe alcohol addiction and PTSD caused by multiple deployments and a hidden life fabricated on a shame spiral. Along with this physical victory, he also won the gift of authenticity to launch a new life—Mark 2.0. Mark jokes that if he were on tour, it would be called the Looks Like We Made It Tour.

Gibson re-entered the workforce, applying authenticity strategies and techniques to every facet of his new life. Landing a job familiar to his expertise in public relations, Mark moved back to the United States and took a job with the U.S. Small Business Administration in Atlanta, Georgia. Before long, Mark was tapped by SBA Headquarters to co-author and lead a National LGBT Outreach initiative with the National Gay & Lesbian Chamber of Commerce®. LGBT Business Builder would be recognized by the White House and become the gold standard for LGBT inclusion in the federal government. LGBT Business Builder received recognition from Harvard University and became the recipient of the Bright Ideas – Innovations in American Government Award.

In addition to being a world traveler and gourmet cook, Mark is a triathlete, a runner, and has a spirit of volunteerism. He is passionate about living an authentic life to its fullest. He and his partner Aaron (a.k.a. "Mr. Wonderful") enjoy living in Georgia and split their time between Midtown Atlanta, Lake Oconee, and their Airbnb in Savannah.